The Journal
of Christopher Columbus

Translated by Cecil Jane
with an appendix by R. A. Skelton

Ninety illustrations from
prints and maps of the period

 Bramhall House
New York

Contents

List of Illustrations

Black and white Illustrations

Western portion of the world map by Juan de la Cosa, 1500. Museo Naval, Madrid

Western portion of the 'Cantino' world map., 1502. Biblioteca Estense, Modena

Part of the world map by G. M. Contarini, engraved in 1506 by Rosselli. The British Museum

Part of a MS world map drawn about 1508. The British Museum (MS Eg. 2803)

Map of the Caribbean; published with Peter Martyr's first *Decade of the New World*, 1511

Map of the New World; in Ptolemy, *Geographia*, Strassburg, 1513

The Western Hemisphere in the world map by Franciscus Monachus; in *De orbis situ*, Antwerp, 1529

Map of the Western Hemisphere drawn about 1535. The British Museum (MS Sloane 117)

Foreword

When Christopher Columbus returned from his first voyage to America and was received by Ferdinand and Isabel in Barcelona, he presented them with the holograph original of his log-book, which he had kept from day to day. The Sovereigns did not return the manuscript to Columbus, but retained it. In exchange, by order of Isabel, a copy was sent to the admiral shortly before he sailed on his second voyage. This copy had been made by two scribes in the utmost secrecy, to prevent Portuguese spies from gaining knowledge of its contents.

Columbus and his descendants must have treasured the Barcelona manuscript and must have kept it in the family archives. It was probably this copy which Luis Columbus, Christopher's grandson, had in his possession in 1554, when he was granted permission to publish the *Journal*; but for some unknown reason the project was not carried out. The *Journal* was not printed, and we shall never know its full contents, since both the holograph original and the Barcelona copy have disappeared.

The only text of Columbus' diary which has come down to us is an abstract in the hand of the Dominican historian Bartolomé de las Casas. It may be that Las Casas used the Barcelona copy to make his abstract, for he was well acquainted with several members of the Columbus family, particularly with Christopher's sons, Diego and Fernando, and with Diego's wife, Doña Maria de Toledo. Through them he may have had access to the family archives. It appears more likely, however, that he made use of a transcript of the Barcelona manuscript, which he found in Fernando's library.

Fernando Columbus, a man of keen intellect, spent his life and income collecting books. At his death, his library contained more than fifteen thousand volumes and many valuable manuscripts. In his will (1539), he left his library to his nephew Luis, with the provision that if the latter showed no inclination to provide for the upkeep of the library, it should be turned over to the chapter of the Seville cathedral. At the time, Luis was under age and residing in Santo Domingo; he could do nothing about the inheritance. But in 1544 his mother, Maria de Toledo — probably acting on the suggestion of her brother Antonio, who was a Dominican — entrusted the care of Fernando's library to the Dominican monastery of San Pablo. Las Casas resided in this monastery when he was in Seville. It was there that he was consecrated Bishop of Chiapas on March 30, 1544; but he was unable then to make much use of Fernando's library, as it was not transferred to San Pablo until June of that year, and four weeks later, Las Casas, Maria de Toledo and her brother Antonio sailed from Sanlúcar de Barrameda for Santo Domingo.

In 1552, however, Las Casas spent most of the year in the monastery of San Pablo. The library was still there, although the chapter of the Seville cathedral had obtained a court order for its transfer; but the library was not moved until the end of the year. This was a year of feverish activity for Las Casas. He supervised the printing of several of his works, and he also began to redact his *opus magnum*, the *Historia de las Indias*, which he did not complete until six years later, in Valladolid.

Before beginning to write his *Historia*, like any conscientious historian Las Casas collected material and took notes. Naturally a very important source of information for him was Columbus' diary. From the manuscript which he found in Fernando's library, he copied word for word those parts which he thought of special interest, and abridged other sections which seemed less important. To correct errors or to elucidate doubtful points, he added a considerable number of marginal notes. He also copied an account of Columbus' third voyage.

Several historians have accused Las Casas of tampering with the spirit of the *Journal*, of falsifying its contents to suit his own views. The first critic to do so was Henry Vignaud. In 1930 Cecil Jane amplified Vignaud's arguments, asserting that the letter-prologue which precedes the *Journal* is a forgery and that Columbus could not have written it, since in it Ferdinand and Isabel are addressed as "King and Queen of the Spains," a title which was not used until later, when the union of Castile and Aragon became permanent. But Jane's argument cannot be sustained, for as early as 1488 the court chronicler, Pedro Martir de Anghiera, in his correspondence, addressed Isabel as "Queen of the Spains" and her son and heir as "Prince of the Spains." If Pedro Martir used such a title in 1488, there is no reason why Columbus could not have done the same four years later.

The most outspoken critic of Las Casas has been the Argentinian scholar Romulo Carbia. At the *Congrès International des Américanistes*, held in Seville in 1935, Carbia indulged in violent diatribes against the Dominican, calling him a liar and a forger. His accusations aroused strong reactions, but failed to make converts. Today's leading authorities on Las Casas, such as Lewis Hanke and Manuel Jiménez Fernández, are of the opinion that Las Casas did not alter the spirit of Columbus' diary.

There is no doubt, however, that Las Casas did introduce some remarks of his own into the text of the *Journal*, but he did so in good faith and did not intend to attribute them to Columbus. The reference to Florida (on November 21st) could not be the work of Columbus, since that province was not discovered until 1513. It was evidently added by Las Casas. The historian Henry Harrisse also thought that some of the place names given in the *Journal* probably belong to a later period. Among others, Harrisse mentions Cabo Francés, on the north shore of Santo Domingo. The original name given by Columbus appears to have been Cabo Franco, which is found on the map drawn by La Cosa in 1500. This map is preserved in the Museo Naval in Madrid.

The *Journal* also contains a number of errors of transcription which may be the work of Las Casas, or which he may have found in the manuscript from which he made his abstract. Several of these errors concern navigation and make it difficult to follow the course set by Columbus. They usually consist in mistaking *este* (east) for *oeste* (west), or in giving the distances in leagues instead of miles, or vice-versa. Other errors seem to be just slips of the pen, such as writing *teniendo* for *temiendo* (October 13th) or *soldar* for *sondar* (November 28th). There are also lacunae and some unintelligible passages, probably due to missing lines and words. In several instances Las Casas experienced considerable difficulty in deciphering the text of the *Journal*, which he blamed on the bad handwriting of the scribe.

If Las Casas did not alter the log-book, did Columbus himself do so? Did he revise his own *Journal* after his return to Spain, to correct his errors or to give it a particular slant? This is very unlikely. S. E. Morison has pointed out that when the admiral realized that he had been mistaken days or weeks before, he made no effort to correct his errors, but let them stand in the *Journal*. When Martin Alonso Pinzón deserted on November 21st, Columbus gave vent to his feelings, and in the entry for that day he included some very critical remarks about his chief subordinate. Yet his praise of Martin Alonso in the early pages of his diary were allowed to remain. This and other aspects of the *Journal* show that it was written from day to day, as a log-book, and that it suffered no revision by the admiral.

Las Casas often found cause to criticize the language and style of Columbus. In his *Historia de las Indias*, after quoting word for word from the *Journal*, the Dominican sometimes added remarks like this: "These are his very words, although some of them are not in perfect Castilian, since it was not the admiral's mother tongue." Las Casas evidently thought that the foreign terms or constructions used by Columbus must have been Italian in origin, since he was from Genoa. Yet in all of his writings we find hardly a trace of the Italian language. His letters addressed to Genoese friends or to the Banco di San Giorgio are written in Spanish. All of the marginal notes found in his own copy of Pliny's *Natural History* are written in Spanish, except one which is in very bad Italian. Spanish was the language in which Columbus felt most at home when he had to set down his thoughts on paper.

The foreign words which Columbus detected in the *Journal* were probably Portuguese in origin, for Menéndez Pidal and Sá Nogueira have noticed a large number of "portuguesismos" in the admiral's language. This is not surprising in view of the fact that he spent seven years in Portugal, Madeira and Porto Santo. His knowledge of Portuguese appears to have been largely oral; he does not seem to have ever learned to write it well, and he did not handle it as if it were his native tongue. Columbus lived at a time when the linguistic frontier between Portuguese and Castilian was vague and hard to define, and most of his "portuguesismos" appear in spelling and pronunciation. For some words common to both languages, he used only the Portuguese spelling, while for others he wrote the Portuguese or Castilian form indifferently. Some of his technical terms relating to navigation may be Portuguese, if they do not belong to the "language of the galleys," the *lingua franca* common to sailors of southwestern Europe. Thus *barlovento* (windward) and *sotavento* (leeward), *nordestar* (to decline to the northeast) and *noroestar* (to decline to the northwest) may be Portuguese in origin, if they are not derived from some other romance language.

Julio Guillén y Tato, director of the Museo Naval in Madrid, has made an interesting study of Columbus' nautical language. This study reveals that while in the early pages of the *Journal* the nautical terms are few in number, they progressively increase in the successive entries. From this the Spanish scholar derives the impression that before 1492 Columbus was unfamiliar with the jargon of the Spanish sailors; but as he was intelligent and adaptable, he quickly learned the language of the sea.

In the early part of his *Journal*, Columbus uses the Arabo-Portuguese word *almadia* when he wishes to refer to the Indian dugout. Later, however, when he has learned the native word for it (canoa), he begins to make use of it. Other Americanisms which Columbus introduced in Europe through his log-book are *cacique* (local chieftain or leader), *hamaca* (hammock) and *tiburón* (shark). Today these words are an integral part of the Spanish language. During his first voyage Columbus became acquainted with tobacco, but he did not learn the word for it.

The style of the *Journal* is matter of fact and devoid of literary flourishes, except for reminiscences of the Bible, Pliny the Elder and Mandeville. When Columbus asked the Indians whether the monsters described by Mandeville were to be found in the Indies, the natives, who did not understand him, nodded assent, and the admiral concluded that such monsters peopled some of the islands, although he failed to see any of them. The *Travels of John Mandeville* enjoyed wide credit in the later Middle Ages; but their author was a first class liar who related a lot of tall tales about countries he had never visited.

Columbus may not have known too much about astronomy and the use of nautical instruments (when he tried to take the latitude with his quadrant the result was usually far from accurate); but his dead reckoning was uncanny, particularly if we consider the fact that he was navigating in totally unknown waters. His knowledge of flora and fauna was limited, and most of his identifications of trees and plants are only approximate. The nightingales which he thought he heard in Española were probably mocking birds.

Like many of his contemporaries, Columbus was imbued with a deep, naive faith. While searching for gold, pearls and precious stones, he also showed concern for the spiritual welfare of the natives, and he thought that they could be easily converted since they seemed to have no creed of their own. In his great undertaking he was thoroughly convinced that God was on his side and even performed miracles on his behalf. Thus on his outward journey, when the sailors began to complain about the smooth sea and the lack of wind (September 23rd), fearing that under such conditions they would never be able to return to Spain, the sea suddenly rose and the waves swelled, and the men stopped grumbling. The admiral interpreted this event as an act of the Divine Providence and compared it to the miracle of the Red Sea, when gigantic waves destroyed Pharaoh's army after the Jews had reached land and safety.

In addition to his *Journal*, Columbus also wrote a letter giving a condensed account of his first voyage. It is dated February 15, 1493, and was written on board during the homeward voyage. It was the custom for Spanish admirals and captains to put their papers and accounts in order and to attend to official correspondence a few days before landing. The Archivo de Indias in Seville contains many such letters written by high officials returning from America.

Unlike the *Journal*, whose text remained secret, the letter was immediately given wide publicity. As early as April of 1493 it was printed in Barcelona, and one month later a Latin version was published in Rome. During the next four years editions of it appeared in Valladolid, Basle, Antwerp, Paris and Strassbourg, in Spanish, Latin, French and German; and a rhymed version was published in Italian in Florence. Fernando Columbus had a copy of a Catalan translation in his library, but this has since disappeared. The Spanish bibliophile Carlos Sanz has recently published facsimiles of seventeen editions of the letter, all published before 1500.

In these editions, the letter is addressed either to Gabriel Sánchez or to Luis de Santangel, both high officials of the Kingdom of Aragon; but the contents do not vary. It seems that Columbus used the same text for at least five letters, which he addressed to the Sovereigns, Gabriel Sánchez, Luis de Santangel, the Duke of Medinaceli and the Cordoba town council. All these letters were probably sent from Lisbon, with the possible exception of the one for Cordoba, which he may have dispatched from Palos after he landed there on March 15, 1493. We know that this letter was read to a meeting of the Cordoba aldermen on March 22nd, and its bearer was rewarded with a thousand maravedis in cash and a new suit. In addition, the courier probably brought other messages of a private nature, for Cordoba was Columbus' home in Spain and he had left there his mistress, Beatriz de Arana, and his two sons, Diego and Fernando, who were attending school. Furthermore, two of the men whom Columbus had left behind in Santo Domingo were from Cordoba: one was Diego de Arana, cousin of Beatriz; the other was the physician Juan Sánchez. The messenger may have brought messages from them to their relatives.

The Journal, on the other hand, remained unknown for centuries. In 1791 Martin Fernández de Navarrete discovered the Las Casas abstract in the library of the Duke del Infantado, and published it in 1825 in the first volume of his *Colección de Viajes*. Navarrete had served in the Spanish navy, and in his edition of the *Journal*, he corrected some obvious errors relating to navigation. But he was not a trained paleographer, and his transcription contains a number of misreadings. A more satisfactory edition of the *Journal* was included in the first volume of the *Raccolta Colombiana* in 1892. It was the work of Cesare de Lollis, chief editor of the *Raccolta*, and of Julian Paz, archivist of the House of Alba. The *Raccolta* edition is by no means perfect, as Professor Emiliano Jos has pointed out, but it is textually superior to Navarrete's.

Since the end of the Spanish civil war, the *Journal* has enjoyed considerable popularity in the Hispanic world, and no less than five editions of it have appeared in the last twenty years. The most useful is that prepared by Julio Guillén, which contains valuable footnotes. Another is a de luxe edition, beautifully illustrated, with an introduction by the late Gregorio Marañon. All these editions follow Navarrete's transcription.

The earliest English translation of the *Journal* appeared in 1827. It has been followed by a number of others, the best known being those of Markham, Thacher and Cecil Jane. In 1939 Rinaldo Caddeo published an Italian version of the Journal, which soon afterwards was retranslated into French and German.

None of these foreign versions is entirely satisfactory, for the task of translating the text of the *Journal* into another language requires an almost encyclopaedic mind. It is not enough to have a commanding knowledge of fifteenth century Spanish; only a person who also knows history, geography, astronomy, navigation, flora, fauna, Indian customs, etc., can faithfully convey to foreign readers the letter and spirit of the *Journal*. In an article published in 1939, S. E. Morison has pointed out many of the pitfalls into which English translators of the *Journal* have fallen.

Instead of retranslating the *Journal* from beginning to end, I have used as a basis the Cecil Jane translation, which is the best of the English versions. Jane, a professor at Oxford University, had a fine command of the Spanish language, but he knew little about navigation, fauna and flora. Furthermore, his untimely death kept him from revising his translation, from correcting obvious errors and reinserting missing lines. No doubt he would have achieved a more satisfactory result if he had had the time to complete it. His version of the letter is an excellent example of what a translation should be.

In preparing this edition, instead of using the text printed by Navarrete in 1825, as most translators have done, I have relied on the transcription made in 1892 by Cesare de Lollis and Julian Paz for the *Raccolta Colombiana*, which is far superior. I have also checked doubtful readings with the Las Casas manuscript, now in the Biblioteca Nacional in Madrid. For the sake of clarity I have added footnotes where the text seemed to require it. For identification of place names, I have relied chiefly on Morison, but I have also consulted the work of Julio Guillén, Morales Pedroso and others. I have also added a bibliography of books and articles dealing with the *Journal*.

I wish to express my gratitude for greatly facilitating my task to the staffs of the Archivo General de Indias in Seville, the Sociedade de Geografia in Lisbon, and the Museo Naval in Madrid. Professor M. Jiménez Fernández of the University of Seville has generously provided me with much useful information concerning the whereabouts of Bartolomé de las Casas in 1544 and 1552. Comandante A. Teixeira da Mota of the Portuguese Naval Academy, Almirante Julio Guillén, director of the Museo Naval, and Teniente de Navio Roberto Barreiro-Meiro, also of the Museo Naval, have been most kind in helping me grasp the meaning of nautical terms found in the *Journal*; I am greatly indebted to them for this, since I am not a specialist in such matters. And my deepest graitude goes to Mr. R. A. Skelton, whose moral support and valuable suggestions have never failed me.

L. A. VIGNERAS

The Journal of Christopher Columbus

This is the First Voyage, and the courses and the way, that the Admiral Don Christopher Columbus pursued when he discovered the Indies, set forth in the form of a summary, save for the Prologue, which he addressed to the Sovereigns and which is given in full, and which begins in this manner:

"In the Name of Our Lord Jesus Christ.

"Most Christian and most exalted and most excellent and most mighty princes, King and Queen of the Spains and of the islands of the sea, our Sovereigns: Forasmuch as, in this present year of 1492, after that Your Highnesses had made an end of the war with the Moors who reigned in Europe, and had brought that war to a conclusion in the very great city of Granada, where, in this same year, on the second day of the month of January, I saw the royal banners of Your Highnesses placed by force of arms on the towers of the Alhambra, which is the citadel of the city, and I saw the Moorish king come out of the gates of the city and kiss the royal hands of Your Highnesses and of the Prince, My Lord, and afterwards in that same month, on the ground of information which I had given to Your Highnesses concerning the lands of India, and concerning a prince who is called 'Grand Khan,' which is to say in our Romance tongue 'King of Kings,' how many times he and his ancestors had sent to Rome to beg for men learned in our holy faith, in order that they might instruct him therein, and how the Holy Father had never made provision in this matter, and how so many nations had been lost, falling into idolatries and taking to themselves doctrines of perdition, and Your Highnesses, as Catholic Christians and as princes devoted to the holy Christian faith and propagators thereof, and enemies of the sect of Mahomet and of all idolatries and heresies, took thought to send me, Christopher Columbus, to the said parts of India, to see those princes and peoples and lands and the character of them and of all else, and the manner which should be used to bring about their conversion to our holy faith, and ordained that I should not go by land to the eastward, by which way it was the custom to go, but by way of the west, by which down to this day we do not know certainly that any one has passed; therefore, after having driven out all the Jews from your realms and lordships, [1] in the same month of January, Your Highnesses commanded me that, with a sufficient fleet, I should go to the said parts of India and for this accorded to me great rewards and ennobled me so that from that time henceforward I might style myself 'don' and be high admiral of the Ocean Sea and viceroy and perpetual governor of the islands and continent which I should discover and gain and which from now henceforward might be discovered and gained in the Ocean Sea, and that my eldest son should succeed to the same position, and so on from generation to generation. And I departed from the city of Granada on the twelfth day of the month of May in the same year of 1492, on a Saturday, and came to the town of Palos, which is a port of the sea, where I made ready three ships, very suited for such an undertaking, and I set out from that port, well furnished with very many supplies and with many seamen, on the third day of the month of August of the same year, on a Friday, half an hour before the rising of the sun, and I steered my course for the Canary Islands of Your Highnesses, which are in the Ocean Sea, thence to set out on my way and to sail until I should arrive in the Indies, and deliver the embassy of Your

Fernãd᷈º rex hyspania

Ferdinand of Spain; in the illustrated edition of the Columbus letter, 1493.

Highnesses to those princes and perform all that you had commanded me to do. To this end, I thought to write all this journey very carefully, from day to day, all that I might do and see and experience, as will be hereafter seen. Moreover, Sovereign Princes, in addition to writing each night that which the day had brought forth and each day how I had sailed at night, I design to make a new chart for navigation, in which I will set all the sea and lands of the Ocean Sea in their true places, under their bearings, and moreover to compile a book and to set down all, picturing everything by latitude from the equinoctial line and by longitude from the west; and above all it is very fitting that I should forget sleep and give much attention to navigation, because it should be so. And these things will be a great labour.

"FRIDAY, AUGUST 3rd / On Friday, the third day of August, of the year 1492, at eight o clock, we set out from the bar of Saltés. [2] We went with a strong sea-breeze sixty miles to the southward, that is, fifteen leagues, before sunset; [3] afterwards, to the south-west and south by west which was the course for the Canaries."

SATURDAY, AUGUST 4th / They went to the south-west by south.

SUNDAY, AUGUST 5th / They went on their way, day and night together, more than forty leagues.

MONDAY, AUGUST 6th / The rudder of the caravel *Pinta*, in which was Martin Alonso Pinzón, [4] jumped out of gear; this was believed or suspected to be due to the action of a certain Gomez Rascón and Cristóbal Quintero, to whom the caravel belonged, [5] because that voyage was irksome to him. And the admiral says that, before they set out, these men had been found to be inclined to oppose and pick holes, as they say. The admiral was then much disturbed because he could not help the caravel without danger to himself, and he says that his anxiety was somewhat relieved because he knew that Martin Alonso Pinzón was a man of courage and of good understanding. Eventually, day and night together, they went twenty-nine leagues.

TUESDAY, AUGUST 7th / The rudder of the *Pinta* again was unshipped and they repaired it, and they went on a course for the

The departure of Columbus from Palos; an engraving by Theodore de Bry.

island of Lanzarote, which is one of the Canary Islands. And they made twenty-five leagues, day and night together.

WEDNESDAY, AUGUST 8th / Among the pilots of the three caravels there were different opinions concerning their position, and the admiral proved to be nearest the truth. He was anxious to go to Grand Canary, in order to leave the caravel *Pinta* there, since she was steering badly

and making water, and he wished to secure another there, if one
were to be found. They were not able to arrive there on that day.

THURSDAY, AUGUST 9th / Until the night of Sunday, the admiral could
not make Gomera, and Martin Alonso, by order of the admiral,
remained off that coast of Grand Canary, because he could not steer.
Afterwards the admiral reached Canary or Tenerife, and with much
labour and care on the part of the admiral, of Martin Alonso and of
the others, they repaired the *Pinta* very well, and eventually they
reached Gomera. They saw a great fire coming from the mountain
of the island of Tenerife, which is remarkably lofty. ⁶ They fitted the
Niña with square sails, for she had been lateen rigged. He returned to
Gomera on Sunday, the second of September, with the *Pinta* repaired.
The admiral says that many honourable Spaniards, inhabitants of the
island of Hierro, who were in Gomera with Doña Inés Peraza, the
mother of Guillem Peraza, who was afterwards first Condé de la
Gomera, ⁷ swore that every year they saw land to the westward of the
Canaries, which is towards the setting sun; and others from Gomera
affirmed exactly the same under oath. ⁸ The admiral here says that he
remembers that, being in Portugal in the year 1484, one from the
island of Madeira came to the king and asked of him a caravel, to go
to this land which he saw, and that this man swore that he saw it
every year and always in the same way. ⁹ He also remembers that they
said the same thing in the islands of the Azores, and that all these
agreed concerning the direction and the manner of appearance and
the size. Having taken in water and wood and meat, and the other
things which the men, whom the admiral had left in Gomera, when he
went to the island of Canary to repair the caravel *Pinta*, had obtained,
finally he set sail from the island of Gomera, with his three caravels,
on Thursday, the sixth day of September.

THURSDAY, SEPTEMBER 6th / He set out on that day in the morning
from the harbour of Gomera and shaped his course to proceed upon
his voyage; and the admiral learned from a caravel, which came from
the island of Hierro, that three caravels of Portugal were cruising
there, in order to take him. This must have been due to the envy
which the king felt because he had gone to Castile. And he went all

that day and night in a calm, and in the morning he found himself
between Gomera and Tenerife.

FRIDAY, SEPTEMBER 7th / All Friday and Saturday, until three
o'clock at night, he was becalmed.

SATURDAY, SEPTEMBER 8th / At three o'clock at night, on the Saturday,
it began to blow from the north-east, and he shaped his route and
course to the west. He shipped much sea over the bows, which made
progress slow, and that day and night he went nine leagues.

SUNDAY, SEPTEMBER 9th / He made fifteen leagues that day, and he
determined to reckon less than he made, in order that the crews might
thus not become disheartened or alarmed if the voyage were lengthy.
In the night he went a hundred and twenty miles, at ten miles an
hour, which is thirty leagues. The sailors steered badly, letting her
fall off to west by north and even to west-north-west; concerning
this the admiral many times rebuked them.

MONDAY, SEPTEMBER 10th / In that day and night, he went sixty
leagues, at ten miles, which is two and a half leagues, an hour. But
he only reckoned forty-eight leagues, in order that the crew might not
be dismayed if the voyage were long.

TUESDAY, SEPTEMBER 11th / That day they sailed on their course,
which was to the west, and they made twenty leagues and more. And
they saw a large piece of the mast of a ship of a hundred and twenty
tons, and they could not secure it. During the night, they went about
twenty leagues, and he reckoned no more than sixteen, for the said
reason.

WEDNESDAY, SEPTEMBER 12th / That day, proceeding on their course,
they made in the night and day thirty-three leagues, counting less for
the said reason.

THURSDAY, SEPTEMBER 13th / In that day and night, following their
course which was west, they went thirty-three leagues, and he reckoned
three or four less. The currents were against them. On this day, at
the beginning of the night, the needles turned north-west, and in the
morning they declined north-east somewhat. [10]

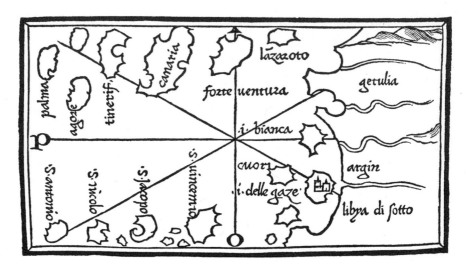

The Canary Islands; in Bordone's *Isolario*, 1528.

FRIDAY, SEPTEMBER 14th / That day they navigated on their course westward, and during the night, and they went twenty leagues. He reckoned somewhat less. Here those in the caravel *Niña* said that they had seen a tern and a tropic-bird; and these birds never go more than twenty-five leagues from land.

SATURDAY, SEPTEMBER 15th / He sailed that day with its night twenty-seven leagues and somewhat more on his westerly course. And on this night, at the beginning of it, they saw fall from the sky a marvellous branch of fire into the sea at a distance of four or five leagues from them.

SUNDAY, SEPTEMBER 16th / He went on his westerly course that day and night. They must have made thirty-nine leagues, but he did not reckon more than thirty-six. That day there were some clouds, a little rain falling. Here the admiral says that then and always after that time they met with very temperate breezes, so that it was a great delight to enjoy the mornings, and nothing was lacking except to hear nightingales. He says: "And the weather was like April in Andalusia." Here they began to see many tufts of very green seaweed, which, as it appeared, had not long been torn from the earth; on this account, all judged that they were near some island, but not to the mainland, according to the admiral, who says: "For the mainland I take to be further on."

MONDAY, SEPTEMBER 17th / He sailed on his westerly course, and they went in the day and night fifty leagues and more: he only counted forty-seven. The current assisted them. They saw much vegetation and it was very delicate and was weed from rocks; and the vegetation came from the westward. They concluded that they were near land. The pilots took the north, marking it, and they found that the needles declined north-west a full point; and the sailors were alarmed and depressed, and they did not say why. When the admiral noticed this, he gave orders that they should mark the north again at dawn, and they found that the needles were true. The explanation was that the star appears to change its position and not the needles. In the morning, on that Monday, they saw much more weed, and it seemed to be grass from rivers, and in this they found a live crab, which the admiral kept. And he says that these were certain signs of land, because they are not found eighty leagues from land. They found that the water of the sea was less salt, after they had left the Canaries, and the breezes constantly softer. They all went on their way greatly rejoicing, and as to the ships, she that could sail fastest went ahead, in order to be the first to sight land. They saw many dolphins, and the crew of the *Niña* killed one. The admiral says here that these indications came from the west: "Where I hope in that high God, in Whose hands are all victories, that very presently He will give us land." On that morning he says that he saw a white bird which is called a tropic-bird, and which is not accustomed to sleep on the sea.

TUESDAY, SEPTEMBER 18th / He navigated that day and night and they made more than fifty-five leagues, but he did not reckon more than forty-eight. All these days, the sea was very smooth, like the river at Seville. On this day Martin Alonso in the *Pinta*, which was a fast sailer, did not wait; for he called to the admiral from his caravel that he had seen a great crowd of birds go towards the west, and hoped to sight land that night, and for this reason he so went ahead. To the northward there appeared a great bank of dark clouds, which is a sign of being near land.

WEDNESDAY, SEPTEMBER 19th / He sailed on his course, and in the day and night went twenty-five leagues, since it was calm. He wrote down twenty-two. This day, at ten o'clock, there came to the ship a booby, and in the evening they saw another, and it is not their habit to go farther than twenty leagues from land. A few drops of rain fell without wind; this is a certain indication of land. The admiral did not wish to be delayed by beating to windward in order to make sure whether there was land in that direction, but he was certain that to the north and to the south there were some islands, as in truth there were, and he went through the midst of them, because his wish was to press onward towards the Indies. "And there is time enough, for, God willing, on the return voyage, all will be seen." These are his words. Here the pilots gave their position. The pilot of the *Niña* made it four hundred and forty leagues from the Canaries; the pilot of the *Pinta*, four hundred and twenty; the pilot of the vessel in which the admiral was, four hundred exactly.

THURSDAY, SEPTEMBER 20th / On this day he navigated west by north and west-north-west because, with the calm which prevailed, the winds were very variable. They must have made some seven or eight leagues. Two boobies came to the ship, and afterwards another, which was a sign that they were near land, and they saw much vegetation, although on the previous day they had seen none. They caught by hand a bird which was like a tern; it was a river, not a sea bird; it had feet like a gull. There came to the ship, at dawn, two or three land birds, singing, and afterwards, before sunset, they disappeared. Afterwards, a booby came; it came from the west-north-west and went south-east, which was an indication that it left land to the west-north-west, for these birds sleep on land and in the morning go out to sea to look for food, and do not fly to a greater distance than twenty leagues.

FRIDAY, SEPTEMBER 21st / Most of that day it was calm, and afterwards there was some wind. They must have gone, day and night together, including the distance which was on their course and that which was not, some thirteen leagues. At dawn, they found so much weed that

Columbus' caravels setting sail from Spain; detail of an engraving of 1621.

the sea appeared to be choked with it, and it came from the west. They saw a booby; the sea was as calm as a river, and the breezes the best in the world. They saw a whale, which is a sign that they were near land, since they always remain near it.

SATURDAY, SEPTEMBER 22nd / He navigated west-north-west, more or less, inclining to one side and to the other. They must have made thirty leagues; they saw hardly any vegetation. They saw some petrels and another bird. Here the admiral says: "This head wind was very necessary to me, since my people were much excited, because they thought that in these seas no winds ever blew to carry them back to Spain." For some part of the day there was no seaweed, afterwards it was very dense.

SUNDAY, SEPTEMBER 23rd / He sailed north-westward and at times northwest by north and at other times keeping to his course, which was to the west. He made some twenty-two leagues. They saw a pigeon and a booby, and another river-bird, and other white birds; there was much vegetation and in it they found crabs. As the sea was calm and smooth, the people murmured, saying that, as there was there no great sea, it would never blow so as to carry them back to Spain. But afterwards the sea, without wind, rose greatly, and this amazed them, for which reason the admiral here says: "So that high sea was very necessary for me, because such a thing had not been seen save in the time of the Jews, when [those] of Egypt came out against Moses who was leading them out of captivity." [11]

MONDAY, SEPTEMBER 24th / He navigated on his course to the west, day and night, and they went fourteen leagues and a half; he reckoned twelve. There came to the ship a booby, and they saw many petrels.

TUESDAY, SEPTEMBER 25th / This day was very calm and afterwards it blew, and they went on their way to the west, until night. The admiral talked with Martin Alonso Pinzón, captain of the other caravel, the *Pinta*, concerning a chart which three days before he had sent to him to the caravel and in which, as it appears, the admiral had certain islands depicted as being in that sea. [12] And Martin Alonso said that they

The stern of a ship, detail of a woodcut of 1486.

were in that neighbourhood, and the admiral replied that such was his opinion, but the fact that they had not reached them must be due to the currents which had carried the ships north-eastward, and they had not gone as far as the pilots said. Having come to this conclusion, the admiral asked him to send the chart to him, and, when it had been sent on a line, the admiral began with his pilot and sailors to fix his position on it. At sunset, Martin Alonso mounted the poop of his ship and in great delight called the admiral, asking for a reward from him because he had sighted land. The admiral says that, hearing this stated positively, he fell on his knees to give thanks to Our Lord, and Martin Alonso with his men said the *Gloria in excelsis Deo*. The admiral's people did the same, and those in the *Niña* all climbed the mast and into the rigging, and all affirmed that it was land. And the admiral thought the same and that it was at twenty-five leagues distance. Until night they all continued to declare that it was land. The admiral order-ed the course, which was to the west, to be changed and they all made south-westward, where the land had appeared. That day they sailed four and a half leagues to the west and in the night seventeen leagues to the south-west, a total of twenty-one. But he told the men that it was thirteen leagues, since he always pretended to his people that he had made a small distance, in order that the voyage might not appear lengthy to them. In this way he kept two reckonings on that voyage: the smaller which was false, and the greater which was true. The sea was very smooth, so that many sailors went swimming. They saw many dorados [13] and other fish.

WEDNESDAY, SEPTEMBER 26th / He sailed on his course to the west until after midday; then they went to the south-west, until it was found that what they had said was land was not land, but only cloud. They made in the day and night thirty-one leagues, and he reckoned twenty-four to his men. The sea was like a river; the breezes sweet and very soft.

THURSDAY, SEPTEMBER 27th / He kept on his course to the west. He went in the day and night twenty-four leagues; he reckoned to his men twenty leagues. Many dorados came and they killed one; they saw a tropic-bird.

FRIDAY, SEPTEMBER 28th / He kept on his course to the west. They made in the day and night, owing to calms, fourteen leagues; he reckon-ed thirteen. They found little vegetation; they took two dorados, and in the other ships they took more.

SATURDAY, SEPTEMBER 29th / He kept on his course to the west. They went twenty-four leagues; he reckoned twenty-one to his men. Owing to the calms which they experienced, they made little way in the day and night. They saw a bird which is called the frigate-bird, which makes the boobies vomit what they have eaten in order to eat it itself and which maintains itself upon nothing else. It is a sea-bird, but it does not settle on the sea, nor does it go more than twenty leagues from land; there are many of these birds in the Cape Verde Islands. They later saw two boobies. The breezes were very sweet and pleasant, so that he says that nothing was wanting save to hear the nightingale, and the sea was smooth as a river. There afterwards appeared, on three occasions, three boobies and a frigate-bird. They saw much vegetation.

SUNDAY, SEPTEMBER 30th / He kept his course to the west. He went, owing to the calms, in the day and night fourteen leagues; he reckoned eleven. Four tropic-birds came to the ship, which is a great indication of land, since so many birds of one kind being together is a sign that they are not straying or lost. Four boobies were also seen, on two occasions; there was much vegetation. Note that the stars which are called the guards, when night falls, are near the arm on the west side, and when dawn breaks, they are on the line below the arm to the north-east, so that it seems that in the whole night they move only three lines, which are nine hours; and this is the case every night.[14] This the admiral says here. Moreover, at nightfall the needles decline a point north-east, and at daybreak they are right on the [north] star, from which it appears that the star moves as the other stars and that the needles always point truly.

MONDAY, OCTOBER 1st / He kept his course to the west. They made twenty-five leagues; he reckoned twenty leagues to his men. They had a heavy fall of rain. The admiral's pilot on this day at dawn calculated that they had gone from the island of Hierro up to then five hundred and seventy-eight leagues westward. The smaller reckoning, which the admiral showed to the men, made it five hundred and eighty-four leagues, but the true distance, which the admiral calculated and kept secret, was seven hundred and seven.

TUESDAY, OCTOBER 2nd / He kept on his course, night and day, for thirty-nine leagues, to the west; he reckoned to the men a matter of thirty leagues. The sea was always smooth and calm. "To God many thanks be given," the admiral says here. Weed was floating from east to west, contrary to that which was generally the case. Many fish appeared; one was killed. They saw a white bird which seemed to be a gull.

WEDNESDAY, OCTOBER 3rd / He followed his ordinary course; they went forty-seven leagues; he reckoned forty leagues to the men. Petrels appeared; there was much vegetation, some very faded and others very fresh and bearing something like fruit. They did not see any birds, and the admiral believed that they had left behind the islands which he had depicted on his chart. The admiral says here that it had not been his wish to keep beating about during the past week and on the days when he saw so many indications of land, although he had information of certain islands in that region, in order not to delay, since his aim was to pass to the Indies and, if he were to have delayed, he says that it would not have been good judgment.

THURSDAY, OCTOBER 4th / He kept on his course to the west; they went, day and night together, sixty-three leagues; he reckoned forty-six to his men. There came to the ship more than forty petrels in a body, and two boobies, and a boy in the caravel hit one with a stone. A frigate-bird come to the ship and a white bird like a gull.

FRIDAY, OCTOBER 5th / He kept on his course; they made eleven miles an hour and in the night and day they went fifty-seven leagues, since during the night the wind freshened somewhat. He reckoned forty-five to his men. The sea was calm and smooth. "To God," he says, "many thanks be given." The air was very sweet and temperate; there was no vegetation; birds, many petrels. Many flying-fish flew into the ship.

SATURDAY, OCTOBER 6th / He kept on his course westwards; they went forty leagues in the day and night; he reckoned thirty-three to his men. On this night Martin Alonso said that it would be well to steer south-west by west, and the admiral thought that Martin Alonso did

Flying fish; an engraving by Theodore de Bry.

not say this on account of the island of Cigangu;[15] and the admiral saw that, if they missed it, they would not be able to reach land so soon, and that it was better to go at once to the mainland and afterwards to the islands.

SUNDAY, OCTOBER 7th / He kept on his course to the west; they made twelve miles an hour for two hours, and afterwards eight miles an hour; and up to an hour after sunrise he went twenty-three leagues. He reckoned eighteen to his men. On this day, at sunrise, the caravel *Niña*, which went ahead as she was a fast sailer, and they all went as

quickly as they could in order to be the first to sight land and secure
the reward which the Sovereigns had promised to whomsoever should
first sight it, hoisted a standard at the mast-head and fired a lombard,
as a sign that they saw land; for so the admiral had ordered. He had
also ordered that, at sunrise and at sunset, all the ships should join
him, since these are the two periods when it is most possible to see
for a distance, the mists clearing. In the evening the land, which those
in the *Niña* thought they had seen, was not sighted, and a great flock
of birds passed from the direction of the north to the south-west, which
led him to believe that they were going to sleep on land or were, perhaps,
flying from the winter which was about to come to the lands whence
they came. As the admiral knew that most of the islands which the
Portuguese held had been discovered through birds, on this account
the admiral decided to abandon the westward course and to steer west-
south-west, [16] with the resolve to proceed in that direction for two days.
He began to do so one hour before sunset. They made in the whole
night a matter of five leagues, and twenty-three in the day; in the
night and day together, they went in all twenty-eight leagues.

MONDAY, OCTOBER 8th / He navigated west-south-west, and day and
night together they went about eleven and a half or twelve leagues,
and it seems that at times in the night they made fifteen miles an hour,
if the text be not corrupt. They had a sea like the river of Seville.
"Thanks be to God," says the admiral, "the breezes were softer than
in April at Seville, so that it is a pleasure to be in them: they are so
laden with scent." The vegetation seemed to be very fresh; there were
many land birds, and they took one, and they were flying to the
south-west, terns and ducks and a booby.

TUESDAY, OCTOBER 9th / He sailed south-westward; he made five leagues. The wind changed and he ran to the west by north, and went
four leagues. Afterwards, in all, he made eleven leagues in the day
and in the night twenty and a half leagues; he reckoned seventeen
leagues to the men. All night they heard birds passing.

WEDNESDAY, OCTOBER 10th / He navigated west-south-west; they
made ten miles an hour and at times twelve and sometimes seven, and

Mariner's astrolabe; Spanish, sixteenth century.

in the day and night together they went fifty-nine leagues; he reckoned to the men forty-four leagues, no more. Here the men could now bear no more; they complained of the long voyage. But the admiral heartened them as best he could, holding out to them bright hopes of the gains which they could make, and he added that it was vain for them to complain, since he was going to the Indies and must pursue his course until, with the help of Our Lord, he found them.

THURSDAY, OCTOBER 11th / He navigated to the west-south-west; they had a rougher sea than they had experienced during the whole voyage. They saw petrels and a green reed near the ship. Those in the caravel *Pinta* saw a cane and a stick, and they secured another small stick, carved, as it appeared, with iron, and a piece of cane, and other vegetation which grows on land, and a small board. Those in the caravel *Niña* also saw other indications of land and a stick loaded with barnacles. At these signs, all breathed again and rejoiced. On this day, to sunset, they went twenty-seven leagues. After sunset, he steered his former course to the west; they made twelve miles an hour, and up to two hours before midnight they had made ninety miles, which are twenty-two leagues and a half. And since the caravel *Pinta* was swifter and went ahead of the admiral, she found land and made the signals which the admiral had commanded. This land was first sighted by a sailor called Rodrigo de Triana,[17] although the admiral, at ten o'clock in the night, being on the sterncastle, saw a light. It was, however, so obscured that he would not affirm that it was land, but called Pero Gutierrez, butler of the King's dais, and told him that there seemed to be a light, and that he should watch for it. He did so, and saw it. He said the same also to Rodrigo Sanchez de Segovia, whom the King and Queen had sent in the fleet as *veedor*,[18] and he saw nothing since he was not in a position from which it could be seen. After the admiral had so spoken, it was seen once or twice, and it was like a small wax candle, which was raised and lowered. Few thought that this was an indication of land, but the admiral was certain that they were near land. Accordingly, when they had said the *Salve*, which all sailors are accustomed to say and chant in their manner, and when they had all been gathered together, the admiral asked and urged them to keep a good look out from the forecastle and to watch carefully for land, and to him who should say first that he saw land, he would give at once a silk doublet apart from the other rewards which the

Sovereigns had promised, which were ten thousand maravedis annually to him who first sighted it. Two hours after midnight land appeared, at a distance of about two leagues from them. They took in all sail, remaining with the mainsail, which is the great sail without bonnets, and kept jogging, waiting for day, a Friday, on which they reached a small island of the Lucayos, which is called in the language of the Indians "Guanahaní." [19] Immediately they saw naked people, and the admiral went ashore in the armed boat, and Martin Alonso Pinzón and Vicente Yañez, his brother, who was captain of the *Niña*. The admiral brought out the royal standard, and the captains went with two banners of the Green Cross, which the admiral flew on all the ships as a flag, with an F and a Y, and over each letter their crown, one being on one side of the ✷ and the other on the other. When they had landed, they saw very green trees and much water and fruit of various kinds. The admiral called the two captains and the others who had landed, and Rodrigo de Escobedo, secretary of the whole fleet, [20] and Rodrigo Sanchez de Segovia, and said that they should bear witness and testimony how he, before them all, took possession of the island, as in fact he did, for the King and Queen, his Sovereigns, making the declarations which are required, as is contained more at length in the testimonies which were there made in writing. Soon many people of the island gathered there. What follows are the actual words of the admiral, in his book of his first voyage and discovery of these Indies.

"I," he says, "in order that they might feel great amity towards us, because I knew that they were a people to be delivered and converted to our holy faith rather by love than by force, gave to some among them some red caps and some glass beads, which they hung round their necks, and many other things of little value. At this they were greatly pleased and became so entirely our friends that it was a wonder to see. Afterwards they came swimming to the ships' boats, where we were, and brought us parrots and cotton thread in balls, and spears and many other things, and we exchanged for them other things, such as small glass beads and hawks' bells, which we gave to them. In fact, they took all and gave all, such as they had, with good will, but it seemed to me that they were a people very deficient in everything. They all go naked as their mothers bore them, and the women also, although I saw only one very young girl. And all those whom I did see were youths, so that I did not see one who was over thirty years of age; they were very well built, with very handsome bodies and very good faces. Their hair is coarse almost like the hairs of a horse's tail and short; they wear their hair down over their eyebrows, except for a few strands behind, which they wear long and never cut. Some of them are painted black, and they are the colour of the people of the Canaries, neither black nor white, and some of them are painted white and some red and some in any colour that they find. Some of them paint their faces, some their whole bodies, some only the eyes, and some only the nose. They do not bear arms or know them, for I showed to them swords and they took them by the blade and cut themselves through ignorance. They have no iron. Their spears are certain reeds, without iron, and some of these have a fish tooth at the end, while others are pointed in various ways. They are all generally fairly tall, good looking and well proportioned. I saw some who bore marks of wounds on their bodies, and I made signs to them to ask how this came about, and they indicated to me that people came from other islands, which are near, and wished to capture them, and they defended themselves. And I believed and still believe that they come here from the mainland to take them for slaves. They should be good servants and of quick intelligence, since I see that they very soon say all that is said to them, and I believe that they would easily be made Christians, for it appeared to me that they had no creed. Our Lord willing, at the time of my departure I will bring back six of them to Your Highnesses, that they may learn to talk. I saw no beast of any kind in this island, except parrots." All these are the words of the admiral.

"SATURDAY, OCTOBER 13th / As soon as day broke, there came to the shore many of these men, all youths, as I have said, and all of a good height, very handsome people. Their hair is not curly, but loose and coarse as the hair of a horse; all have very broad foreheads and heads, more so than has any people that I have seen up to now. Their eyes are very lovely and not small. They are not at all black, but the colour of Canarians, and nothing else could be expected, since this

The landing on Española; an engraving by Theodore de Bry.

is in one line from east to west with the island of Hierro in the Canaries. Their legs are very straight, all alike; they have no bellies but very good figures. They came to the ship in boats, which are made of a tree-trunk like a long boat and all of one piece. They are very wonderfully carved, considering the country, and large, so that in some forty or forty-five men came. Others are smaller, so that in some only a solitary man came. They row them with a paddle, like a baker's peel, and they travel wonderfully fast. If one capsizes, all at once begin to swim and right it, baling it out with gourds which they carry with them. They brought balls of spun cotton and parrots and spears and other trifles, which it would be tedious to write down, and they gave all for anything that was given to them. And I was attentive and laboured to know if they had gold, and I saw that some of them wore a small piece hanging from a hole which they have in the nose, and from signs I was able to understand that, going to the south or going round the island to the south, there was a king who had large vessels of it and possessed much gold. I endeavoured to make them go there, and afterwards saw that they were not inclined for the journey. I resolved to wait until the afternoon of the following day, and after that to leave for the south-west, for, as many of them indicated to me, they said that there was land to the south and to the south-west and to the north-west, and that those of the north-west often came to attack them. So I resolved to go to the south-west, to seek the gold and precious stones. This island is fairly large and very flat; the trees are very green and there is much water. In the centre of it, there is a very large lake; there is no mountain, and all is so green that it is a pleasure to gaze upon it. The people also are very gentle and, since they long to possess something of ours and fear that nothing will be given to them unless they give something, when they have nothing, they take what they can and immediately throw themselves into the water and swim. But all that they do possess, they give for anything which is given to them, so that they exchange things even for pieces of broken dishes and bits of broken glass cups. I even saw one give sixteen balls of cotton for three *ceotis* of Portugal, which are a Castilian *blanca*, and in these balls there was more than an *arroba* of spun cotton. [21] I should forbid this and should not allow anything to be taken, unless it be that I command all, if there be a quantity, to be taken for Your Highnesses. It grows here in this island, but owing to lack of time, I can give no definite account; and here is also produced that gold which they wear hanging from the nose. But, in order not to lose time, I wish to go and see if I can make the island of Cipangu. Now, as it was night, they all went to land in their boats."

"SUNDAY, OCTOBER 14th / At dawn, I ordered the ship's boat and the
boats of the caravels to be made ready, and I went along the island
in a north-north-easterly direction, to see the other part, which lay to
the east, and its character, and also to see the villages. And I soon saw
two or three, and the people all came to shore, calling us and giving
thanks to God. Some brought us water, others various eatables: others,
when they saw that I was not inclined to land, threw themselves into
the sea and came, swimming, and we understood that they asked us
if we had come from heaven. One old man got into the boat, and all
the rest, men and women, cried in loud voices: 'Come and see the men

Indians flee in fear of Columbus; in Dati's version of the Columbus letter, 1493.

who have come from heaven; bring them food and drink.' Many came and many women, each with something, giving thanks to God, throwing themselves on the ground and raising their hands to the sky, and then shouting to us that we should land. But I feared to do so, seeing a great reef of rocks which encircled the whole of that island, while within there is deep water and a harbour large enough for all the ships of Christendom, the entrance to which is very narrow. It is true that inside the reef there are some shoals, but the sea is no more disturbed than the water in a well. And in order to see all this, I went this morning, that I might be able to give an account of all to Your Highnesses and also say where a fort could be built. I saw a piece of land, which is formed like an island although it is not one, on which there were six houses; it could be converted into an island in two days, although I do not see that it is necessary to do so, for these people are very unskilled in arms, as Your Highnesses will see from the seven whom I caused to be taken in order to carry them off that they may learn our language and return. However, when Your Highnesses so command, they can all be carried off to Castile or held captive in the island itself, since with fifty men they would be all kept in subjection and forced to do whatever may be wished. Near the said islet, moreover, there are the loveliest groups of trees that I have ever seen, all green and with leaves like those of Castile in the month of April and May, and much water. I examined the whole of that harbour, and afterwards returned to the ship and set sail. I saw so many islands that I could not decide to which I would go first. Those men, whom I had taken, made signs to me that there were very many, so many that they could not be counted, and they mentioned by name more than a hundred. Finally I sought for the largest and resolved to steer for it, which I am doing. It is five leagues away from this island of San Salvador, and of the others, some are more and some less distant. All are very flat, without mountains, and very fertile; all are inhabited and they make war upon one another, although these people are very simple and very well formed men."

"MONDAY, OCTOBER 15th / I stood off that night, fearing to come to anchor before daylight, as I did not know whether the coast was free from shoals. At daybreak, I hoisted sail. And as the island was more than five leagues distant, being rather about seven, and the tide was against me, it was about midday when I arrived at the island. I found that the side which lies towards the island of San Salvador runs north and south for a distance of five leagues, and that the other side, which I followed, runs east and west for more than ten leagues. And as from this island I saw another and larger to the west, I set sail to go all that day until night, since otherwise I should not have been able to have reached the westerly point. To this island I gave the name *Santa Maria de la Concepción,* [22] and about sunset, I anchored off the said point to learn if there were gold there, because those whom I had caused to be taken in the island of San Salvador told me that there they wore very large golden bracelets on the legs and arms. I can well believe that all that they said was a ruse in order to get away. It was nevertheless my wish not to pass any island without taking possession of it, although when one had been annexed, all might be said to have been. And I anchored and was there until to-day, Tuesday, when at dawn I went ashore in the armed boats and landed. The people, who were many, were naked and of the same type as those of the other island of San Salvador; they allowed us to go through the island and gave us what we asked of them. And as the wind blew more strongly across from the south-east, I was unwilling to wait and went back to the ship. A large canoe was alongside the caravel *Niña,* and one of the men of the island of San Salvador, who was in her, threw himself into the sea and went off in it, and during the evening before midnight the other threw himself overboard . . ., [23] and went after the canoe, which fled so that there was not a boat that could have overtaken it, since we were a long way behind it. In the end it reached land and they left the canoe, and some of my company went ashore after them, and they all ran off like chickens. The boat which they had abandoned we brought on board the caravel *Niña.* To her, there now came from another direction another small canoe with a man who wished to barter a ball of cotton, and some sailors jumped into the sea and took him, because he would not come on board the caravel. I was on the poop of the ship and saw everything, and I sent for him and gave him a red cap and some small beads of green glass, which I put on his arm, and two hawks' bells, which I put in his ears, and ordered his canoe, which was also in the ship's boat, to be given back to him and sent him ashore. After that I set sail to go to the other large island which I saw to the west. I commanded that the other canoe, which the *Niña* was towing astern, should be set adrift also. Afterwards, on land, when the other, to whom I had given the things mentioned and from whom I had refused to take the ball of cotton, although he wished to give it to me, reached it, I saw that all the rest clustered round him and that he was dazzled and quite sure that we were good people and that the one who had run away had somehow wronged us and that accordingly we had carried him off. It was to create this impression that I had so acted with him, ordering him to be set free and giving him the presents, in order that we may be held in his esteem so that when Your Highnesses again send here, they may not be unfriendly. All that I gave to him was not worth four maravedis. [24] So I departed at about ten o'clock, with a south-east wind that veered southerly, in order to pass over to the other island. It is very large and there all these men, whom I carry with me from the island of San Salvador, make signs that there is much gold and that they wear it as bracelets on their arms and on their legs, and in their ears and noses and around their necks. From this island of Santa Maria to the other was some nine leagues, from east to west, and all this side of the island runs from north-west to south-east. It seems that on this side the coast may extend for some twenty-eight leagues or more; the island is very flat, without any mountains, as are San Salvador and Santa Maria, and all the coasts are free from rocks, except that they all have some reefs near the land under water, on which account it is necessary to keep a sharp look out when it is proposed to anchor, and not to anchor very near the shore, although the waters are always very clear and the depth can be seen. At a distance of two lombard shots from land, the water off all these islands is so deep that it cannot be sounded. These islands are very green and fertile and the breezes are very soft, and it is possible that there are in them many things, of which I do not know, because I did not wish to delay in finding gold, by discovering and going about many islands. And since these men give these signs that they wear it on their arms and legs, and it is gold because I showed them some pieces of gold which

mamei.   guaiaua.   guanauana.   platano.

Fruit trees found in the New World; in Benzoni's *Historia del Mondo Nuovo*, 1563.

I have, I cannot fail, with the aid of Our Lord, to find the place whence it comes. Being in the middle of the channel between these two islands, that of Santa Maria and this large island, to which I gave the name *Fernandina*,[25] I found a man alone in a canoe on his way from the island of Santa Maria to that of Fernandina. He was carrying with him a piece of their bread, about as large as the fist, and a gourd of water and a piece of brown earth, powdered and then kneaded, and some dried leaves, which must be a thing highly prized among them, since already at San Salvador they presented me with some of them. He also carried with him a basket of their make, in which he had a string of glass beads and two blancas, through which I knew that he came from the island of San Salvador and had crossed to that of Santa Maria and was on his way to Fernandina. He came alongside the ship. I made him come on board, as he asked to do so, and caused him to bring his canoe on board also and all that he had with him to be kept safe. I commanded that bread and honey should be given to him to eat, and something to drink, and thus I will carry him to Fernandina and will give him back all his belongings, in order to give him a good opinion of us, so that when, please God, Your Highnesses send here, those who come may receive honour and the Indians will give to us of all that they have."

"TUESDAY AND WEDNESDAY, OCTOBER 16th / I departed from the islands [26] of Santa Maria de Concepción when it was already about mid-day for that of Fernandina, which loomed very large to the westward, and I navigated all that day in a calm. I could not arrive in time to be able to see the bottom in order to anchor in a clear place, for it is necessary to exercise great care in this matter so as not to lose the anchors, and accordingly I stood off and on all that night until day when I came to a village, where I anchored and from which had come the man whom I had found the day before in that canoe in the middle of the channel. He had given so good a report of us that all that night there was no lack of canoes alongside the ship; they brought us water and what they had. I ordered something to be given to each of them, that is to say, some small beads, ten or a dozen of glass on a string, and some brass timbrels, of the kind which are worth a maravedi each in Castile, and some leather thongs; [27] all these things they regarded as most excellent. When they came on board the ship, I also commanded molasses to be given to them to eat. And afterwards, at the hour of terce, [28] I sent the ship's boat ashore for water, and they with good will showed my people where the water was and themselves carried the full casks to the boat, and they were delighted to give us pleasure. This island is very large, and I am resolved to round it, because, as far as I can understand, there is in it or near it a gold mine. This island is distant from that of Santa Maria about eight leagues, almost from east to west, and this point, where I came, and all this coast runs north-north-west and south-south-east; I saw quite twenty leagues of it, but it did not end there. Now, as this is being written, I have set sail with a south wind in order to try to round the

whole island and go on until I find Samoet, which is the island or
city where there is gold, for so say all those who came on board the
ship here, and so those from the island of San Salvador and from that
of Santa Maria have told us. These people are like those of the said
islands and have the same speech and manners, except that these here
seem to me to be somewhat more domesticated and tractable, and more
intelligent, because I see that they have brought here cotton to the ship
and other trifles for which they know better how to bargain than the
others did. And in this land also I saw cotton cloths made like mantil-
las, and the people are better disposed and the women wear in front of
their bodies a small piece of cotton, which scarcely hides their secret
parts. This island is very green and flat and very fertile, and I have no
doubt that all the year they sow and reap Indian corn, and equally
other things. I saw many trees very unlike ours, and many of them had
many branches of different kinds, and all coming from one root; one
branch is of one kind and one of another, and they are so unlike each
other that it is the greatest wonder in the world. How great is the
difference between one and another! For example: one branch has
leaves like those of a cane and another leaves like those of a mastic
tree, and thus, on a single tree, there are five or six different kinds all
so diverse from each other. They are not grafted, for it might be said
that it is the result of grafting; on the contrary, they are wild and these
people do not cultivate them. No creed is known to them and I believe
that they would be speedily converted to Christianity, for they have a
very good understanding. There are here fish, so unlike ours that it
is a marvel; there are some shaped like dories, of the finest colours in
the world, blue, yellow, red and of all colours, and others painted in
a thousand ways, and the colours are so fine that no man would not
wonder at them or be anything but delighted to see them. There are
also whales. I saw no land animals of any kind, except parrots and
lizards. A boy told me that he saw a large snake. I did not see any
sheep or goats or other animals, but I have been here a very short while,
as it is now midday. None the less, if there had been any I could not
have failed to see one. I will describe the circuit of this island when
I have rounded it."

"WEDNESDAY, OCTOBER 17th / I set out from the village at midday from my anchorage and from where I had taken water in order to round this island of Fernandina, and the wind was south-west and south. It was my wish to follow the coast of this island, from where I was to the south-east, because it all trended north-north-west and south-south-east, and I desired to take the route to the south-south-east, because in that direction, as all the Indians whom I have with me say and as another indicated, towards the south, lies the island which they call Samoet, where there is gold. And Martin Alonso Pinzón, captain of the caravel *Pinta*, in which I sent three of these Indians, came to me and told me that one of them had very definitely given him to understand that the island could be rounded more quickly in a north-north-westerly direction. I saw that the wind would not help me for the course which I wished to steer and that it was favourable for the other course, and I sailed north-north-west. And when I was about two leagues from the head of the island, I found a very wonderful harbour with a mouth, or rather it may be said with two mouths, since there is an islet in the middle, and both mouths are very narrow, and within it is more than wide enough for a hundred ships, if it be deep and clear and there be depth at the entrance. I thought it well to examine it closely and to take soundings, and so I anchored outside it, and went into it with all the ships' boats, and we saw that it was shallow. And as I thought, when I saw it, that it was the mouth of a river, I had ordered casks to be brought to take water, and on land I found some eight or ten men, who immediately came to us and showed us a village near there, where I sent the people for water, some of them with arms and some with casks, and so they took it. And as it was some distance away, I was kept there for the space of two hours. During this time I walked among the trees, and they were the loveliest sight that I have yet seen; they seemed to be as green as those of Andalusia in the month of May, and all the trees are as different from ours as day is from night, and so is the fruit and the grasses and the stones and everything else. It is true that some trees were of the kind that are found in Castile, but yet there is a great difference, and there are many other kinds of trees which no one could say are like or can be compared with those of Castile. All these people are like those already

Trading with the Indians; in the illustrated edition of the Columbus letter, 1493.

mentioned. They are of the same type and as naked and of the same height, and they give what they have for whatever is given to them. And here I saw that some boys from the ships exchanged some little pieces of broken dishes and glass for their spears. The others, who went for the water, told me how they had been in their houses and that inside they were thoroughly swept and clean, and that their beds and coverings are like nets of cotton. They, that is the houses, are all like tents and very high and with good chimneys, [29] but among the many villages which I have seen, I have not seen one of more than from twelve to fifteen houses. Here they found that married women wore cotton drawers, but girls did not, except some who were already eighteen years old. There are here mastiffs and small dogs, and here they found a man who had in his nose a piece of gold, which might have been half the size of a castellano, on which they saw letters. [30] I was angry with them because they had not bargained for it and given whatever might be asked, in order that it might be examined and seen what money it was, and they replied to me that they had not dared to bargain for it. After the water had been taken, I returned to the ship and set sail, navigating so far to the north-west that I discovered all that part of the island until the coast runs east and west. And afterwards all these Indians repeated that this island was smaller than the island of Samoet and that it would be well to turn back in order to arrive at it sooner. There the wind presently fell and then began to blow from the west-north-west, which was contrary for the course which we had been following. I therefore turned back and navigated all that night in an east-south-easterly direction, sometimes due east and sometimes south-east; this was done in order to keep clear from the land, because there were very thick clouds and the weather was very heavy. There was little wind and this prevented me from coming to land to anchor. Then this night it rained very heavily from after midnight until near daybreak, and it is still cloudy with a threat of rain. We are at the end of the island to the south-east, where I hope to anchor until the weather clears, so that I can see the other islands to which I propose to go. So it has rained, more or less, every day since I have been in these Indies. Your Highnesses may believe that this is the best and most fertile and temperate and level and good land that there is in the world."

"THURSDAY, OCTOBER 18th / When the weather had cleared, I sailed before the wind and continued the circuit of the island when I could do so, and anchored when it was not well to navigate. But I did not land, and at dawn I set sail."

"FRIDAY, OCTOBER 19th / At dawn I weighed anchor and sent the caravel *Pinta* to the east-south-east, and the caravel *Niña* to the south-south-east, while I in the ship went to the south-east. I gave orders that they should follow these courses until midday, and that both should then change their course and rejoin me. And presently, before we had sailed for three hours, we saw an island to the east, towards which we steered, and all the three vessels reached it before midday, at its northern point, where there is an islet and a reef of rocks on its seaward side to the north and another between it and the main island. These men from San Salvador, whom I have with me, called this island 'Samoet,' and I named it *Isabella*.[31] There was a north wind, and

A Spanish ship; a woodcut of 1496.

the said islet lay on the course from the island of Fernandina, from
which I had navigated from east to west. Afterwards the coast ran from
that islet to the west and extends for twelve leagues to a cape, which
I named *Cape Hermoso*. [32] It is on the west coast and it is indeed lovely,
round and in deep water, with no shoals off it. At first the shore is
stony and low, and further on there is a sandy beach which is character-
istic of most of that coast, and there I anchored this night, Friday,
until morning. All this coast, and the part of the island which I saw,
is mainly a beach; the island is the loveliest thing that I have seen, for,
if the others are very lovely, this is more so. It has many trees, very
green and tall, and this land is higher than the other islands which
have been discovered. There is in it one elevation, which cannot be
called a mountain, but which serves to beautify the rest of the island,
and it seems that there is much water there in the centre of the island.
On this north-eastern side, the coast curves sharply, and is very thickly
wooded with very large trees. I wished to go to anchor there, in order
to land and to see such beauty, but the water was of little depth and I
could only anchor at a distance from the shore, and the wind was very
favourable for reaching this point where I am now lying at anchor, and
which I have named Cape Hermoso, because such it is. So I did not
anchor within that curve and also because I saw this cape, so green and
lovely, at a distance. All the other things and lands of these islands are
so lovely that I do not know where to go first, and my eyes never weary
of looking at such lovely verdure so different from that of our own
land. I believe, moreover, that here there are many herbs and many
trees which will be of great value in Spain for dyes and as medicinal
spices, but I do not recognise them and this causes me much sorrow.
When I arrived here at this cape, there came from the land the scent of
flowers or trees, so delicious and sweet, that it was the most delightful
thing in the world. In the morning, before I go from here, I will land
to see what there is here at this point. There is no village, except further
inland, where these men, whom I have with me, say that there is a king
and that he wears much gold. To-morrow I wish to go so far inland to
find the village and to see or have speech with this king, who, according
to the signs which these men make, rules all these neighbouring islands
and is clothed and wears on his person much gold, although I do not

put much trust in what they say, both because I do not understand them well and because they are so poor in gold that any small amount which this king may wear would seem to be much to them. This point here I call Cape Hermoso. I believe that it is an island separated from that of Samoet, and even that there is another small island between them. I make no attempt to examine so much in detail, since I could not do that in fifty years, because I wish to see and discover as much as I can, in order to return to Your Highnesses in April, if it please Our Lord. It is true that, if I arrive anywhere where there is gold or spices in quantity, I shall wait until I have collected as much as I am able. Accordingly I do nothing but go forward in the hope of finding these."

"SATURDAY, OCTOBER 20th / To-day, at sunrise, I weighed anchor from the place where I was with the ship, anchored off the south-west point of this island of Samoet, to which point I gave the name *Cape de la Laguna* [33] and to the island that of Isabella, in order to steer to the north-east and east from the south-east and south. For there, as I understood from these men whom I have with me, was the village and its king. I found the water everywhere so shallow that I could not enter or navigate to that point, and I saw that, following the route to the south-west, it would be a very great detour. Therefore I determined to return by the way which I had come, to the north-north-east from the west, and to round this island in that direction, and the wind was so light that I was unable ever to proceed along the coast except in the night, and as it is dangerous to anchor off these islands except in daytime, when it is possible to see with the eye where to let go the anchor, since the bottom varies everywhere, some part being clean and some not, I proceeded to stand off under sail all this Sunday night. The caravels anchored, because they found themselves near land earlier, and they thought that from the signals which they were in the habit of making, I should come to anchor, but I did not wish to do so."

"SUNDAY, OCTOBER 21st / At ten o'clock I arrived here at this *Cape del Isleo* [34] and anchored, as did the caravels. After having eaten, I went ashore, and there was there no village but only a single house, in which I found no one, so that I believe that they had fled in terror, because in the house were all their household goods. I allowed nothing to be touched, but only went with these captains and people to examine the island. If the others, which have been already seen, are very lovely and green and fertile, this is much more so, and has large and very green trees. There are here very extensive lagoons, and by them and around them there are wonderful woods, and here and in the whole island all is as green and the vegetation is as that of Andalusia in April. The singing of little birds is such that it seems that a man could never wish to leave this place; the flocks of parrots darken the sun, and there are large and small birds of so many different kinds and so unlike ours, that it is a marvel. There are, moreover, trees of a thousand types, all with their various fruits and all scented, so that it is a wonder. I am the saddest man in the world because I do not recognise them, for I am very sure that all are of some value, and I am bringing specimens of them and also of the herbs. As I was thus going round one of these lagoons, I saw a snake, which we killed, and I am bringing its skin to Your Highnesses. When it saw us, it threw itself into the lagoon and we went in after it, for the water was not very deep, until we killed it with our spears.   It is seven palms in length;[35] I believe that there are many similar snakes here in these lagoons. Here I recognised the aloe, and to-morrow I am resolved to have ten quintals brought to the ship, since they tell me that it is very valuable. Further, going in search of very good water, we arrived at a village near here, half a league from where I am anchored. The inhabitants, when they saw us, all fled and left their houses and hid their clothing and whatever they had in the undergrowth. I did not allow anything to be taken, even the value of a pin. Afterwards, some of the men among them came towards us and one came quite close. I gave him some hawks' bells and some little glass beads, and he was well content and very joyful. And that this friendly feeling might grow stronger and to make some request of them, I asked him for water; and, after I had returned to the ship, they came presently to the beach with their gourds full, and were delighted to give it to us, and I commanded that another string of small glass beads should be given to them, and they said that they would come here to-morrow. I was anxious to fill all the ships' casks with water here; accordingly, if the weather permit, I shall presently set out to

An Indian canoe; in Oviedo's *La hystoria generale de las Indias*, 1547.

go round the island, until I have had speech with this king and have seen whether I can obtain from him the gold which I hear that he wears. After that I wish to leave for another very large island, which I believe must be Cipangu, according to the signs which these Indians whom I have with me make; they call it 'Colba.' They say that there are ships and many very good sailors there. Beyond this island, there is another which they call 'Bofio,' which they say is also very large.[36] The others, which lie between them, we shall see in passing, and according to whether I shall find a quantity of gold or spices, I shall decide what is to be done. But I am still determined to proceed to the mainland and to the city of Quisay[37] and to give the letters of Your Highnesses to the Grand Khan, and to request a reply and return with it."

"MONDAY, OCTOBER 22nd / All this night and to-day I have been here, waiting to see if the king of this place or other personages would bring gold or anything else of importance. There did come many of these people, who were like the others in the other islands, just as naked and just as painted, some white, some red, some black, and so in various ways. They brought spears and some skeins of cotton to exchange, and they bartered these with some sailors for bits of glass from broken cups and for bits of earthenware. Some of them wore some pieces of gold, hanging from the nose, and they gladly gave these for a hawks' bell, of the kind made for the foot of a sparrow-hawk, and for glass beads, but the amount is so small that it is nothing. It is true that whatever little thing might be given to them, they still regarded our coming as a great wonder, and they believed that we had come from heaven. We took water for the ships in a lagoon which is here near Cape del Isleo, for so I named it. And in the lagoon, Martin Alonso Pinzón, captain of the *Pinta*, killed another snake, like that of yesterday, seven palms long; and here I caused to be collected as much aloe as was found."

"TUESDAY, OCTOBER 23rd / I wished to-day to set out for the island of Cuba, which I believe must be Cipangu, according to the indications which these people give me concerning its size and riches. I did not delay longer here or . . . round this island to go to the village, as I had determined, to have speech with this king or lord, in order not to delay too long, since I see that here there is no gold mine, and since to round these islands there is need of various winds, and it does not blow just as men may wish, and since it is well to go where there is much business. I say that it is not right to delay, but to go on our way and to discover much land, until a very profitable land is reached. My impression, however, is that this is very rich in spices, but I have no knowledge of these matters, which causes me the greatest sorrow in the world, for I see a thousand kind of trees, each one of which bears fruit after its kind and is as green now as in Spain in the months of May and June, and a thousand kind of herbs, also in bloom. And in all this I recognise only the aloe, of which I have ordered much to be brought to the ship to carry to Your Highnesses. I have not set nor am I setting sail for Cuba, because there is no wind, but a dead calm, and it is raining heavily and it rained heavily yesterday, without being at all cold. On the contrary, the day is hot and the nights mild as in May in Spain in Andalusia."

"WEDNESDAY, OCTOBER 24th / This night, at midnight, I weighed anchor from the island of Isabella, from Cape del Isleo, which is on the north side where I had stayed, for the island of Cuba, which I hear from these people is very large and has much trade, and has in it gold and spices and great ships and merchants, and they

indicated to me that I should steer west-south-west to go there. This
I am doing, for I believe that, if it be as all the Indians of these islands
and those whom I carry with me in the ships give me to understand
by signs, for I do not know their language, it is the island of Cipangu,
of which marvellous things are recounted; and in the spheres which
I have seen and in the drawings of mappemondes, it is in this region.
And I navigated until day to the west-south-west, and at dawn the
wind fell and it rained, and so it was almost all night. I was thus with
little wind until after midday, and then it began to blow very gently,
and I set all my sails on the ship, the mainsail and two bonnets, and the
foresail and spritsail, the mizen, main topsail and the boat's sail on the
poop. So I went on my course until nightfall, when Cape Verde, in the
island of Fernandina, which is on the south side in the western part,
lay to my north-west, and was seven leagues distant from me. And as
it now blew hard, and I did not know what distance it was to the island
of Cuba, and in order not to go in search of it at night, because all these
islands lie in very deep water, so that no bottom can be found beyond
two lombard shots' distance, and then it is all patchy, one part being
rocky and another sandy, and hence it is impossible to anchor safely,
except when it is possible to see, I decided to take in all sail, except the
foresail, and to proceed under it. After a short while, the wind became
much stronger and I made a considerable distance, at which I felt
misgivings, and as there were thick clouds and it was raining, I ordered
the foresail to be furled, and that night we went less than two leagues," etc.

THURSDAY, OCTOBER 25th / After sunrise, until nine o'clock, he navigated to the west-south-west. They made five leagues. Afterwards he
changed the course to the west. He went eight miles an hour, until an
hour after midday, and from then until three o'clock, and they went
forty-four miles. Then they sighted land and it was seven or eight
islands in a row, all lying north and south. They were five leagues
distant from them, etc.

FRIDAY, OCTOBER 26th / He was to the south of the said islands. It
was everywhere shallow water for five or six leagues. He anchored
there; the Indians whom he carried with him said that from these

islands to Cuba it was a journey of a day and a half for their boats,
which are small vessels of a single piece of wood, carrying no sail.
These are canoes. He set out from there for Cuba, because from the
signs which the Indians made to him concerning its greatness and
its gold and pearls, he thought that it was that land, that is to say,
Cipangu.

SATURDAY, OCTOBER 27th / They weighed anchor at sunrise from
those islands, which he called *Las Islas de Arena*,[38] on account of the
little depth of water which there was to the south of them for a distance
of six leagues. He made eight miles an hour to the south-south-west
until one o'clock and they went about forty miles, and by nightfall
they had gone twenty-eight miles more on the same course, and before
night they saw land. They spent the night on watch while it rained
heavily. On Saturday, up to sunset, they went seventeen leagues to
the south-south-west.

SUNDAY, OCTOBER 28th / He went from there in search of the
nearest point in the island of Cuba to the south-south-west, and he
entered a very lovely river, very free from danger of shoals or of
other obstacles, and the water all along the coast, where he went,
was very deep and clear up to the shore. The mouth of the river
was twelve fathoms deep, and it is fully wide enough to beat about.
He anchored, as he says, a lombard shot within it. The admiral
says that he had never seen anything so beautiful. All the neighbourhood of the river was full of trees, lovely and green, and different
from ours, each one with flowers and fruit after its kind; there were
many birds and small birds, which sang very sweetly. There were a
great number of palms, different from those of Guinea and from ours,
of moderate height, and their feet had no bark, and the leaves were
very large; they cover their houses with them. The land is very flat.
The admiral jumped into the boat and went to shore, and he came
to two houses, which he believed to be those of fishermen, who fled
in terror. In one of them he found a dog that never barked, and in
both houses he found nets of palm fibre and lines and horn fish-hooks,
and bone harpoons, and other fishing-tackle, and many fires in the
houses. He believed that in each one of the houses many persons lived

together. He commanded that none of these things should be touched, and so it was done. The vegetation was as abundant as in Andalusia in April and May. He found much purslane and wild amaranth. He returned to the boat and went a good distance up the river, and it was, as he says, so great a joy to see that verdure and the trees and to hear the singing of the birds that he could not leave it to return.

He says that the island is the most lovely that eyes have ever seen; it is full of good harbours and deep rivers, and it seems that the sea can never be stormy, for the vegetation on the shore runs down almost to the water, which it does not generally do where the sea is rough. Up to that time, he had not experienced a high sea among all those islands. He says that the island is full of very beautiful mountains, although there are no very long ranges, but they are lofty, and all the rest of the land is high like Sicily. It is full of many waters, as he was able to gather from the Indians whom he carried with him and whom he had taken in the island of Guanahani; they told him by signs that there are ten large rivers, and that they cannot go round it in their canoes in twenty days. When he went near the shore with the ships, two boats or canoes came out, and as they saw that the sailors entered the boat and rowed about in order to see the depth of the river, to know where they should anchor, the canoes fled. The Indians said that in that island there are gold mines and pearls; the admiral saw that the place was suited for them, and that there were mussels, which are an indication of them. And the admiral understood that the ships of the Grand Khan come there, and that they are large; and that from there to the mainland it is ten days' journey. The admiral called that river and harbour *San Salvador*.[39]

MONDAY, OCTOBER 29th / He weighed anchor from that harbour and navigated to the west in order, as he says, to go to the city where he thought that the Indians told him that the king resided. One point of the island ran out six leagues to the north-west; from there another point ran out to the east ten leagues. He went another league, and saw a river with a smaller mouth, to which he gave the name *Rio de la Luna*.[40] He went on until the hour of vespers. He saw another river, much larger than the former, and so the Indians told him by signs, and near it he saw fair villages of houses. He called the river the *Rio de Mares*.[41] He sent two boats to a village to have speech, and in one of them an Indian of those whom he carried with him, because by now they understood something and showed themselves to be well pleased with the Christians. All, men, women and children, fled from these houses, abandoning them with all that they had, and the admiral

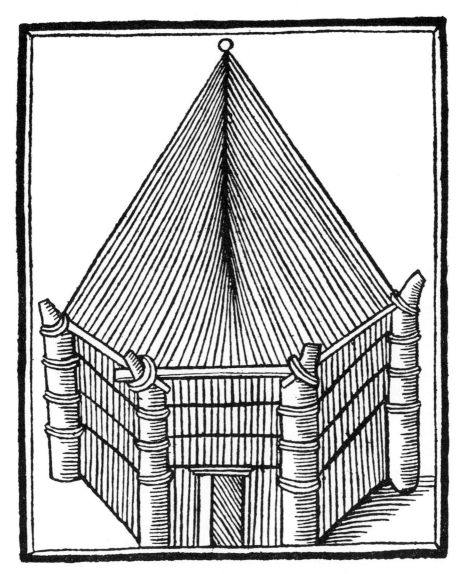

An Indian habitation; in Oviedo's *La hystoria generale de las Indias*, 1547.

commanded that nothing should be touched. The houses, so he says, were quite the most lovely that they had seen, and he believed that the nearer they came to the mainland, the better they would be. They were made in the manner of tents, very large, and they looked like tents in a camp, with no regular streets, but one here and another there. Inside, they were well swept and clean, and their furnishing very well arranged; all were made of very beautiful palm branches. They found many images made like women and many heads like masks, very well worked. He did not know if they had them for their beauty or whether they worship them. There were dogs that never bark; there were wild birds, tamed, in their houses; there were wonderful outfits of nets and hooks and fishing-tackle. They did not touch any of these things. He believed that all those on the coast must be fishermen who carry the fish inland, for that island is very large and so lovely, that he was never weary of speaking well of it. He says that he found trees and fruit with a very wonderful taste, and he says that there should be in it cows and other herds, since he saw skulls which seemed to be those of cows. [42] There are birds, large and small, and the chirping of the crickets went on all night, at which all were delighted; the air all night was scented and sweet, and neither cold nor hot. And further, on the voyage from the other islands to that island, he says that there was great heat, and that in this island there was not, but it was as temperate as May. He attributes the heat of the other islands to the fact that they are very flat and that the wind there blows from the south and is thus warm. The water of those rivers was salt at the mouth; they did not know where the Indians found drinking water, although they had fresh water in their houses. In this river the ships could turn to go in and go out, and they have very good signs or landmarks. The water was seven or eight fathoms deep at the mouth and five within. All that sea, as he says, seems to him to be always as calm as the river of Seville, and the water suited for the cultivation of pearls. He found large periwinkles, tasteless and not like those of Spain. He described the character of the river and the harbour, which he mentioned above and which he named *San Salvador*, as having lovely mountains near and lofty as la Peña de los Enamorados. [43] One of them has on its summit another peak, like a beautiful mosque. This river and harbour, in which he then was, has on the south-east side two quite round mountains and on the west-north-west side a lovely flat cape which projects outwards.

TUESDAY, OCTOBER 30th / He went from the Rio de Mares to the north-west and saw a cape full of palms, and he named it *Cape de Palmas*.⁴⁴ After having gone fifteen leagues, the Indians who were in the caravel *Pinta* said that behind that cape there was a river, and that from the river to Cuba it was four days' journey. The captain of the *Pinta* said he understood that this Cuba was a city, and that land was a very extensive mainland which stretched far to the north, and that the king of that land was at war with the Grand Khan, whom they called "cami," and his land or city they called "Saba" and by many other names. The admiral resolved to go to that river and send a present to the king of the land, and send him the letter of the Sovereigns. For this purpose he had a sailor who had gone to Guinea in the same way, and certain Indians from Guanahani who were ready to go with him, on condition that afterwards they might return to their own land. In the opinion of the admiral, he was distant from the equinoctial line forty-two degrees to the north, if the text from which I have copied this is not corrupt; and he says that he must attempt to go to the Grand Khan, for he thought that he was in that neighbourhood, or to the city of Catay, which belongs to the Grand Khan, which, as he says, is very large, as he was told before he set out from Spain. He says that all this land is low-lying and lovely, and the sea deep.

WEDNESDAY, OCTOBER 31st / All night, Tuesday, he was beating about, and he saw a river where he could not enter because the mouth was shallow, and the Indians thought that the ships could enter as their canoes entered it. And navigating farther on, he found a cape which jutted very far out and was surrounded by shallows, and he saw an inlet or bay, where small vessels might enter, and he could not make it, because the wind had shifted due north and all the coast ran north-north-west and south-east. Another cape which he saw jutted still farther out. For this reason and because the sky showed that it would blow hard, he had to return to the Rio de Mares.

THURSDAY, NOVEMBER 1st / At sunrise, the admiral sent the boats to land, to the houses which were there, and they found that all the people had fled, and after some time a man appeared, and the admiral ordered that he should be allowed to become reassured, and the boats returned to the ships. After eating, he proceeded to send ashore one of the Indians whom he carried with him and who, from a distance, called out to them, saying that they should not be afraid, because these were good people and did harm to no one, and were not from the Grand Khan, but in many islands to which they had been, had given of what they possessed. And the Indian threw himself into the water and swam ashore, and two of those who were there took him by the arms and brought him to a house, where they questioned him. And when they were certain that no harm would be done to them, they were reassured, and presently there came to the ships more than sixteen boats or canoes, with spun cotton and their other trifles, of which the admiral commanded that nothing should be taken, in order that they might know that the admiral sought nothing except gold, which they call "nucay." So all day they were going and coming from the land to the ships, and they went to and fro from the Christians to the shore with great confidence. The admiral did not see any gold among them. But the admiral says that he saw on one of them a piece of worked silver, hanging from the nose, which he took to be an indication that there was silver in that land. They said by signs that within three days many merchants would come from the interior to buy the things which the Christians brought there, and that they would give news of the king of that land, who, as far as he could understand from the signs which they made, was four days' journey from there, because they had sent many men through the whole land to tell of the admiral. "These people," says the admiral, "are of the same character and have the same customs as the others who have been found, having no creed that I know, since up to this moment I have not seen those whom I carry with me offer any prayer, but they say the *Salve* and the *Ave Maria* with their hands raised to heaven, as they are shown, and they make the sign of the cross. There is, moreover, one language for them all, and they are all friends, and I believe that all these islands are so and that they are at war with the Grand Khan, whom they call 'cavila,' and his province 'Basan'; and they all go naked like the others." This the admiral says. He says that the river is very deep and at its mouth they could bring the ships alongside the

land. The fresh water does not come within a league of the mouth
and it is very fresh, and, "It is certain," says the admiral, "that this is
the mainland, and that I am," he says, "before Zayto and Quisay, a
hundred leagues, a little more or less, distant from one and the other,
and this appears clearly from the sea, which is of a different character
from what it has been to the present, and yesterday, going to the north-
west, I found that it was becoming cold."

FRIDAY, NOVEMBER 2nd / The admiral decided to send two men,
Spaniards: one was called Rodrigo de Jerez, who lived in Ayamonte,
and the other was a certain Luis de Torres, who had lived with the
adelantado of Murcia and who had been a Jew, and who, as he says,
understood Hebrew and Chaldee and even some Arabic.[45] With these,
he sent two Indians: one from among those whom he brought with him
from Guanahani, and the other from those houses which were situated
on the river. He gave them strings of beads with which to buy food,
if they were in need of it, and appointed six days as the time within
which they must return. He gave them specimens of spices to see if
they found any, and instructed them how they were to ask for the
king of that land, and what they were to say on behalf of the Sovereigns of Castile, how they had sent the admiral to present letters on
their behalf and a gift. They were also to learn of his estate, establish
friendship with him, and favour him in whatever he might need from
them, etc.; and they should gain knowledge of certain provinces and
harbours and rivers, of which the admiral had information, and learn
how far they were from this place, etc. Here the admiral took the
altitude on this night with a quadrant, and found that he was forty-
two degrees from the equinoctial line,[46] and he says that according to
his estimate, he found that he had gone from the island of Hierro one
thousand one hundred and forty-two leagues, and he still affirms that
this is the mainland.

SATURDAY, NOVEMBER 3rd / In the morning, the admiral entered the
boat, and as the river at its mouth forms a great lake, which makes
a very remarkable harbour, very deep and free from rocks, with an
excellent beach on which to careen ships and with much wood, he
went up the river until he came to fresh water, which was a distance

of some two leagues. And he ascended an eminence, in order to see something of the land, and he could see nothing, owing to the large groves, luxuriant and odorous, on which account he did not doubt that there were aromatic plants. He says that everything he saw was so lovely that his eyes could not weary of beholding such beauty, nor could he weary of the songs of birds, large and small. That day there came many boats or canoes to the ships, to barter articles of spun cotton and the nets in which they sleep, which are hammocks.

SUNDAY, NOVEMBER 4th / Immediately at dawn, the admiral entered the boat and went ashore to hunt some of the birds which he had seen on the previous day. After his return, Martin Alonso Pinzón came to him with two pieces of cinnamon, and said that a Portuguese, whom he had in his ship, had seen an Indian who was carrying two large handfuls of it, but that he did not dare to barter for it, owing to the penalty which the admiral had imposed upon anyone who should barter. He said further that this Indian was carrying some bright red things like nuts. The boatswain of the *Pinta* said he had found cinnamon trees. The admiral immediately went there and found that they were not cinnamon. The admiral showed to some Indians of that place cinnamon and pepper—I suppose some of that which he had brought from Castile as a specimen—and they recognised it, as he says, and indicated by signs that there was much of it near there, towards the south-east. He showed them gold and pearls, and certain old men replied that in a place which they called "Bohio"[47] there was a vast amount, and that they wore it round the neck and on the ears and legs, and also pearls. He further understood that they said that there were large ships and merchandise, and that all this was to the south-east. He also understood that far from there were men with one eye, and others with dogs' noses who ate men, and that when they took a man, they cut off his head and drank his blood and castrated him. The admiral determined to return to the ship to await the two men whom he had sent, intending himself to go in search of those lands if they did not bring some good news of the things they sought. The admiral says further: "These people are very mild and very timorous, naked, as I have said, without arms and without law; these lands are

A pineapple; in Oviedo's *La Hystoria generale de las Indias*, 1547.

very fertile; they are full of *mames*, which are like carrots and which
have the taste of chestnuts;[48] and they have beans and kidney beans very
different from ours and much cotton, which they do not sow, and it
grows wild in great trees; and I believe that the season for gathering
it is all the year round, since I saw bolls open and others about to open
and flowers, all on one tree; and there are a thousand other kinds of
fruit, which it is impossible for me to write down; and all must be
of value." All this says the admiral.

MONDAY, NOVEMBER 5th / At dawn, he ordered the ship beached
for careening, and the other vessels, but not all at the same time,
so that two should always be at the place where they were for safety,
although he says that those people were very confiding and that they
might have beached all the vessels at one time without fear. While

this was going on, the boatswain of the *Niña* came to ask a reward from the admiral, because he had found mastic; but he did not bring a specimen, because he had dropped it. The admiral promised him a reward, and sent Rodrigo Sanchez and master Diego to the trees,[49] and they brought a little of it. He kept it to take back to the Sovereigns, and also a piece of the tree, and he says that he recognised that it was mastic, although it should be gathered at the due season, and in that district there was enough to collect a thousand quintals every year. He found, so he says, a good deal of that wood there which seemed to him to be aloe. He says further that the harbour of Mares is one of the best in the world and has a better climate and milder inhabitants, and since it has a point which is a rocky hillock, it would be possible to establish a fort there, so that, if that place proved to be rich and important, merchants could be there in safety from any other nations. And he says: "May Our Lord, in Whose hands are all victories, order all that is for His service." He says that an Indian told him by signs that the mastic was good for those suffering stomach pains.

TUESDAY, NOVEMBER 6th / Yesterday, in the night, says the admiral, the two men whom he had sent into the interior came back, and they told him that they had gone twelve leagues, as far as a village of fifty houses, where, he says, there would be a thousand inhabitants, since many live in one house. These houses are like very large tents. They said that they had been received with great solemnity, according to their custom, and that all, men and women alike, came to see them, and that they were lodged in the best houses. These people touched them and kissed their hands and feet, wondering at them and believing that they came from Heaven, and so they gave them to understand. They gave them to eat of what they had. They said that when they arrived, the most honourable persons of the village led them by the arms to the chief house, and gave them two chairs on which they seated themselves, and they all sat on the ground around them. The Indian, who went with them, told them how the Christians lived and how they were good people. Afterwards the men went out and the women entered, and sat in the same way round them, kissing their hands and feet, fondling them, trying to find if they were of

Above, the *Niña* with lateen rig; *below*, the *Pinta*. Models after the plans of E. D'Albertis.

flesh and bone like themselves; they asked them to stay there with them for at least five days. They exhibited the cinnamon and pepper and other spices which the admiral had given to them, and the others told them by signs that there was much of it near there, to the south-east, but they did not know if there was any in that place. Having found that there was no indication of any city, they returned, and it was so that if they had been willing to admit those who wished to come, more than five hundred men and women would have come with them, because they thought that they were going back to heaven. There came with them, however, a chief man of the village and his son, and a servant. The admiral spoke with them, doing them much honour. The Indian indicated to him many lands and islands which there were in that neighbourhood. The admiral thought of bringing him to the Sovereigns, and he says that he does not know what the chief imagined—I suppose that he was afraid—and in the darkness of the night he was anxious to go ashore. And the admiral says that since he had the ship on dry land, not wishing to offend him, he let him go; the Indian said that he would return at dawn, but he never came back. On the way the two Christians found many people, who were on their way to their villages, men and women, with a brand in their hands, the herbs for smoking which they are in the habit of using.[50] They found no village of more than five houses on the way, and all gave them the same reception. They saw many kinds of trees and plants and scented flowers; they saw birds of various kinds, different from those of Spain, with the exception of partridges and nightingales which sang, and geese, of which there were many. They saw no four-footed beasts, save dogs which do not bark. The land is very fertile and very cultivated with "mames" and beans and kidney beans very unlike ours; they saw the same Indian corn and a great quantity of cotton gathered and spun and worked, and in one single house they had seen more than five hundred arrobas, and they considered that it would be possible to get four thousand quintals every year. The admiral says that it seems to him that they do not sow it, and that it gives fruit all the year; it is very fine and has a large boll. He says that those people give everything they have for a very low price, and that a great bundle of cotton is given for a lace end, or anything else which

is given for it. "They are," says the admiral, "a people very free from
wickedness and unwarlike; they are all naked, men and women, as
their mothers bore them. It is true that the women wear only a piece of
cotton, large enough to cover their privy parts and no more, and
they are of very good appearance, and are not very black, less so
than those of the Canaries. I hold, most Serene Princes," the admiral
says here, "that having devout religious persons, knowing their language, they would all at once become Christians, and so I hope in Our
Lord that Your Highnesses will take action in this matter with great
diligence, in order to turn to the Church such great peoples and to
convert them, as you have destroyed those who would not confess the
Father and the Son and the Holy Ghost, and after your days, for we
all are mortal, you will leave your realms in a most tranquil state and
free from heresy and wickedness, and you will be well received before
the eternal Creator, Whom may it please to give you long life and great
increase of many kingdoms and lordships, and the will and inclination
to spread the holy Christian religion, as you have done up to this time.
Amen. To-day I refloated the ship and I am preparing to set out on
Thursday in the name of God, and to go to the south-east to seek
for gold and spices and to discover land." All these are the words of
the admiral, who thought to set out on the Thursday, but, as he had
a contrary wind, he was not able to set out until the twelfth day of
November.

MONDAY, NOVEMBER 12th / He left the harbour and river of Mares at
the end of the quarter of dawn, in order to go to an island which the
Indians, whom he carried with him, vigorously affirmed was called
"Babeque,"[51] where they said, according to the signs which they made,
that the people of the place gather gold on the shore at night with
candles, and afterwards, as he says, with a mallet they make bars of it.
To go there, it was necessary to steer to the east by south. After having
gone eight leagues farther along the coast, he found a river, and,
having gone on from there another four leagues, he found another
river, which seemed to be of great volume and larger than any of the
others which he had found. He did not wish to wait or enter any of
them for two reasons: the first and principal was because the weather

and wind were favourable for going in search of the island of Babeque; the other, because, if in it there were some populous or important city near the sea, it would be seen, and to ascend the river small
vessels were needed, and those which he had were not, and so much
time would be lost, and such rivers are a thing to be explored separ-
ately. All this coast was inhabited, especially near the river to which he
gave the name *Rio del Sol.*[52] He said that on the previous Sunday,
the eleventh of November, it had appeared to him that it would be
well to take some persons from that river, in order to carry them
to the Sovereigns, that they might learn our language, in order to discover what there is in the land, and that, on their return, they might
be tongues for the Christians and adopt our customs and the things
of our faith: "Because I saw, as I recognise," says the admiral, "that
these people have no creed and they are not idolaters, but they are very
gentle and do not know what it is to be wicked, or to kill others, or to
steal, and are unwarlike and so timorous that a hundred of them
would run from one of our people, although they jest with them,
and they believe and know that there is a God in Heaven, and they are
sure that we come from Heaven, and they are very ready to repeat
any prayer that we say to them and they make the sign of the cross.
So Your Highnesses should resolve to make them Christians, for I
believe that, if you begin, in a little while you will achieve the
conversion of a great number of peoples to our holy faith, with the
acquisition of great lordships and riches and all their inhabitants for
Spain. For without doubt there is a very great amount of gold in
these lands, so that it is not without reason that these Indians, whom I
carry with me, say that there are places in these islands where they
dig gold and wear it around their necks, in the ears, and on the arms
and legs, and that there are very large bracelets, pearls of great value
and an infinite amount of spices. And by this river of Mares, from
which I departed this night, there is without doubt a very great
quantity of mastic,[53] and more can be had if more be desired,
for the same trees, being planted, readily take root, and they
are many and very large and they have a leaf like the mastic
and fruit, except that it is larger, as are both the trees and the leaf,
as Pliny says, than I have seen in the island of Chios in the archipelago.

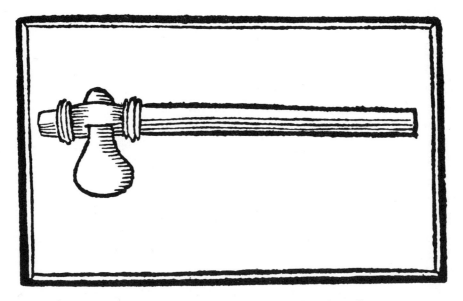

An Indian hatchet; in Oviedo's *La hystoria generale de las Indias*, 1547.

And I ordered many of these trees to be tapped, in order to see if they would give resin to bring back, and as it rained continuously during the time that I was in the said river, I was unable to get any of it, save a very small amount, which I am bringing to Your Highnesses, and it may also be that it is not the season for tapping them, for I believe that the suitable time is when the trees begin to recover from the winter and are about to flower, and here they had fruit which was already almost ripe. And there is also a great amount of cotton here, and I believe that it would be marketed very well here, without bringing it to Spain, taking it only to the cities of the Grand Khan, which will doubtless be discovered, and to the many other cities of other lords who will delight to serve Your Highnesses, and where other things can be supplied from Spain and from the lands of the east, since these lands are to the west of us. And here there is also an infinite amount of aloe, although that is not a thing to produce great gain, but from the mastic much may be expected, since there is none save in the island of Chios, and I believe that they derive from it quite fifty thousand ducats, if my memory does not play me false. And there is here at the mouth of this river the best harbour that I have seen so far, clear and wide and deep, and a good place and situation for making a town and fort, and such that any ships whatever could lie alongside the walls, and the land very temperate and high, and very good waters. It was so that yesterday there came to the side of the ship a boat with six youths, and five came on board the ship; I ordered them to be kept and I will bring them with me. And afterwards I sent to a house which is near the river to the west, and they brought seven head of women, small and large, and three children. I did this, in order that the men might conduct themselves better in Spain, having women of their own land, than if they had not, because already it has many times occurred that men were brought from Guinea, that they might learn the language in Portugal, and afterwards when they had returned it was thought that use might be made of them in their own land, on account of the good company which they had had and the gifts which had been given to them; but when they reached their own land this result never appeared. Others did not so act. So that, having their women, they will be willing to do what is laid upon them, and also these women will do much to teach our people their language, which is one and the same throughout these islands of India, and they all understand one another, and they go all about them in their canoes, which is not the case in Guinea, where there are a thousand differing languages, so that one does not understand the other. This night there came to the side in a canoe the husband of one of these women and father of three children, one male and two female, and asked if I would allow him to come with them and implored me greatly, and they are now all consoled, so that they must all be related. And he is a man of already forty-five years." All these are the exact words of the admiral. He also says above that it was somewhat cold, and for this reason it would not be wise in winter to navigate northwards to discover. On this Monday he sailed before sunset eighteen leagues to the east by south as far as a cape, which he named *Cape Cuba*.[54]

TUESDAY, NOVEMBER 13th / The whole of this night he stood "a la corda," as sailors say, which is to beat to and fro and to make no progress, because he had seen a pass, which is an opening in the mountains, as between one range and another, which began to show at sunset, where two very lofty mountains appeared. It seemed that this was the parting between the land of Cuba and that of Bohio, and this the Indians, whom he carried with him, said by signs. The dawn having come, he made sail for land and passed a point, which at night seemed to him to be some two leagues away, and entered a great gulf, five leagues to the south-south-west, and there remained another five before reaching the cape, where midway between two large mountains there was a cutting, and he could not decide whether or not it was an entrance to the sea.[55] He wished to go to the island which they called "Beneque," where he understood from information he had received, that there was much gold; and that island lay to the east. And since he saw no great centre of population, where he could find shelter against the violence of the wind which rose higher than ever before, he decided to run out to sea and go to the east before the wind which was from the north; and he went eight miles an hour, and from ten o'clock when he took that course until sunset, he went fifty-six miles, which are fourteen leagues, to the east, from Cape Cuba. And of the other land of Bohío, which he left to the leeward, beginning from the cape of the above-mentioned gulf, he discovered, in his opinion, eighty miles, which are twenty leagues. And all that coast runs east-south-east and west-north-west.

WEDNESDAY, NOVEMBER 14th / All the night of yesterday he went cautiously and beating about, because he said that it was not wise to navigate among these islands by night, until they have been examined. For the Indians, whom he had with him, told him yesterday, Tuesday, that it was three days' journey from the Rio de Mares to the island of Baneque, by which must be understood days' journey for their canoes, which are able to go seven leagues. The wind also failed him, and having to go eastward, he could only go east by south, and owing to other obstacles, which he mentions there, he had to wait until morning. At sunrise, he resolved to go in search of a harbour, since the wind had changed from north to north-east, and if he did not find a harbour, it would be necessary for him to go back to the harbours which he had left in the island of Cuba. He reached land, having gone that night twenty-four miles to the east by south; he went south . . . miles to the shore, where he saw many inlets and many islets and harbours. And as the wind was strong, and the sea very rough, he did not dare to attempt the entrance, but ran along the coast to the north-west by west, looking for a harbour, and he saw that there were many, but not very clear. After he had thus gone sixty-four miles, he found a very deep inlet, a quarter of a mile wide, and a good harbour and river, where he entered, and steered to the south-south-west and afterwards south, until he reached the south-east, all very wide and very deep. There he saw so many islands that he could not count them, all of a good size and very high lands, full of various trees of a thousand kinds and an infinity of palms. He marvelled greatly to see so many islands and so lofty, and he assured the Sovereigns that the mountains which he has seen since the day before yesterday, and those of these islands, are in his opinion higher than any in the world, and more lovely and clear, with no cloud or snow, and very great depth of water at their foot. And he says that he believes that these islands are those without number which in the mappemondes are placed at the end of the east. And he said that he believed that in them there were very great riches and precious stones and spices, and that they extend very far to the south, and spread out in every direction. He gave the sea the name *Mar de Nuestra Señora*,[56] and to the harbour which is near the mouth of the entrance to the islands he gave the name *Puerto del Príncipe*. He did not enter it more than to see it from without, until another visit which he made on the Saturday of the following week, as will appear there. He says so many things and so much concerning the fertility and beauty and loftiness of these islands which he found in this harbour, that he tells the Sovereigns that they must not wonder that he praises all so much, because he assures them that he believes he has not said the hundredth part. Some of them seemed to touch the sky, and they were fashioned like diamond points; others, over their highest point, have, as it were, a table on top, and at their foot there is very great depth of water, so that a very large carrack could reach them; they are all full of trees and are not rocky.

Breaming a ship; detail of a woodcut of 1486.

THURSDAY, NOVEMBER 15th / He decided to go among these islands with the ships' boats, and he says marvellous things of them, and that he found mastic and a great quantity of aloe. Some of them were cultivated with the roots from which the Indians make their bread, and he found that fire had been lighted in some places. He did not see fresh water. There were some people and they fled. Everywhere he went, he found a depth of fifteen and sixteen fathoms, and all "basa," which means that the bottom is sand and not rocks, a thing which sailors greatly desire, because the rocks cut the cables of the ships' anchors.

FRIDAY, NOVEMBER 16th / Because in all the places, islands and lands, where he entered, he always left a cross set up, he went into the boat and proceeded to the mouth of these harbours, and on a point of the land he found two very large pieces of timber. One was larger than the other, and the one on top of the other made a cross, so that he says that a carpenter could not have made them better proportioned. And, having adored that cross, he commanded a very great and lofty cross to be made of the same logs. He found canes on that shore, and he did not know where they had grown and believed that some river had carried them down and cast them on the beach; and here he was right. He went to a creek within the entrance of the harbour, to the south-east. A creek is a narrow entrance by which the water of the sea enters into the land. There was there a rocky height and peak like a cape, and at its foot the water was very deep, so that the largest carrack in the world could lie alongside the land, and there was a place or corner, where six ships might lie without anchors as in a hall. It seemed to him that a fort could be made there at small cost, if any considerable trade should develop at any time in that sea of islands. Having returned to the ship, he found the Indians, whom he carried with him, fishing for very large periwinkles which there are in those waters. He made the people dive there and search for *nacaras*, which are the oysters in which pearls are produced. They found many, but no pearls, and he attributed this to the fact that it was not the season for them, which he believed to be May and June. The sailors found an animal which seemed to be a *taso* or *taxo*. [57] They also fished with nets and they found a fish, among many others, which seemed to be a very pig, not like a dolphin, which, he says, was all shell, very hard, and it had no soft place except the tail and eyes, and it had an opening under it to void its superfluities.[58] He ordered it to be salted, in order to take it for the Sovereigns to see.

SATURDAY, NOVEMBER 17th / He entered the boat in the morning and went to examine the islands, which he had not visited, on the south-western side. He saw many others and very fertile and very lovely, and between them there was very great depth of water. Streams of fresh water divided some of them, and he believed that water and those streams originated from some springs which spouted forth in the heights of the mountains of the islands. Going farther on from here, he found a stream very lovely and fresh, and it flowed very cold in its narrow bed. There was a very fair meadow and many very lofty palms, taller than those which he had already seen. I believe that he says that he found large nuts like those of India and also large rats[59] like those of India, and very large crayfish. He saw many birds and there was a strong smell of musk, and he believed that there must be some there. On this day, of the six youths whom he took in the Rio de Mares, and whom he ordered to be kept on the caravel *Niña*, the two oldest escaped.

SUNDAY, NOVEMBER 18th / He went out again in the boats with many people from the ships, and went to set up the great cross which he had ordered to be made from the two logs mentioned, at the mouth of the entrance of the Puerto del Principe, in a prominent position and one free from trees; it was very lofty and a very lovely thing to see. He says that the sea rises and falls there much more than in any other harbour which he has visited in that land, and that it is not surprising considering the many islands, and that the tide is the reverse of ours, because there when the moon is in the south-west by south, it is low tide in that harbour. He did not set out from here, because it was Sunday.

MONDAY, NOVEMBER 19th / He departed before sunrise and with a calm, and afterwards, at midday, it blew somewhat from the east,

and he navigated north-north-east. At sunset, Puerto del Principe lay
to the south-south-west, and was seven leagues distant. He saw the
island of Baneque due east, from which he was distant sixty miles.
He navigated all this night to the north-east; he made rather less than
sixty miles, and up to ten o'clock on the next day, Tuesday, another
twelve, which in all amounts to eighteen leagues, and that to the north-
east by north.

TUESDAY, NOVEMBER 20th / Baneque, or the islands of Baneque, lay
to the east-south-east, from which direction the wind blew so that it
was contrary. Seeing that it did not change and that the sea was rising,
he resolved to return to Puerto del Principe, whence he had set out,
which was twenty-five leagues away. He did not wish to go to the
islet which he called *Isabella*, which was twelve leagues from him,
where he might have reached anchorage that day, for two reasons:
the one, because he saw two islands to the south, which he wished
to examine; the other, because the Indians whom he carried with
him, whom he had taken in Guanahani, which he called San Salvador
and which was eight leagues from that Isabella, might get away, and
he says that he needed them and wanted to take them to Castile, etc.
They had understood, so he says, that, gold being found, the admiral
would allow them to return to their own land. He reached the neighbourhood of Puerto del Principe, but he was unable to make it, as it
was night and as the currents carried him away to the north-west.
He went about and steered to the north-east, with a high wind.
The wind lessened and changed at the third quarter of the night; he
steered to the east by north. The wind was south-south-east, and at
dawn it changed to due south, and veered towards south-east. At sunrise
he was off Puerto del Principe, and it lay to the south-west and almost
south-west by west and he was distant forty-eight miles from it, which
are twelve leagues.

WEDNESDAY, NOVEMBER 21st / At sunrise, he steered to the east with
a south wind; he made little progress, because the sea was against
him. Up to the hour of vespers, he had gone twenty-four miles. Afterwards, the wind changed to the east, and he went to the south by east,

and at sunset he had gone twelve miles. Here the admiral found that he was forty-two degrees from the equinoctial line, to the north, as he had been in the harbour of Mares. But here he says that he has abandoned use of the quadrant until he reaches land, in order that he could repair it. It was accordingly his opinion that he was not so far distant, and he was right, since it was impossible, these islands being only . . . degrees. He was led to believe that the quadrant was correct, as he says, because the north star was as high as in Castile, and if this be true, he had come very near and was as high as Florida. [60] But then where are these islands now which he had close at hand? To this he added that it was, as he said, very hot. But it is clear that if he were off the coast of Florida, he would not have had heat but cold, and it is also manifest that at forty-two degrees it is not to be believed that there is heat in any part of the earth, unless it be for some

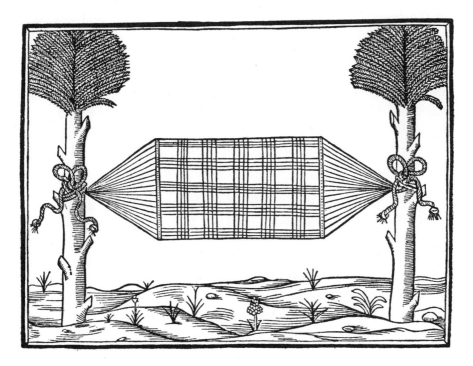

An Indian hammock; in Oviedo's *La hystoria generale de las Indias*, 1547.

accidental reason, and this I do not believe has been known up to the present. From this heat, which the admiral says that he experienced there, he argued that in these Indies and there where he was, there must be much gold. This day Martin Alonso Pinzón, with the caravel *Pinta*, went away, without the permission and against the wish of the admiral, through greed, as he says, thinking that an Indian, whom the admiral had ordered to be placed in that caravel, would give him much gold; and he went away without waiting, without the excuse of bad weather, merely because he wished to do so; and the admiral says here: "He had done and said many other things to me."

THURSDAY, NOVEMBER 22nd / On Wednesday, in the night, he steered to the south by east, with an east wind, and it was almost calm; at the third quarter, it blew from the north-north-east. He was still going southward, in order to examine the land which lay in that direction from him, and when the sun rose, he found himself as far from it as on the previous day, owing to the contrary currents, and the land lay forty miles away from him. On this night, Martin Alonso followed an easterly course, in order to go to the island of Baneque, where the Indians say that there is much gold; he was within sight of the admiral and might have been some sixteen miles away. The admiral sailed within sight of land all night, and he caused some sail to be taken in and kept a lantern alight all night, because it seemed that [Martin Alonso] was coming towards him and the night was very clear and the wind light and good for him to come to him, if he wished.

FRIDAY, NOVEMBER 23rd / The admiral steered all day towards the land to the south, always with a light wind, and the current never permitted him to reach land, but he was to-day as far from it at sunset as he had been in the morning. The wind was east-north-east and satisfactory for going to the south, except that it was light; and beyond this cape there stretched out another land or cape, which also trended to the east, which those Indians whom he had with him called "Bohio." They said that this land was very extensive and that in it were people who had one eye in the forehead, and others whom they called "Cani-bals." Of these last, they showed great fear, and when they saw that this course was being taken, they were speechless, he says, because those people ate them and because they are very warlike. The admiral says that he well believes that there is something in this, but that since they were armed, they must be an intelligent people, and he believed that they may have captured some men and that, because they did not return to their own land, they would say that they were eaten. They believed the same of the Christians and of the admiral, when some first saw them.

SATURDAY, NOVEMBER 24th / He navigated all that night and at nine in the morning he made land at the level island, the same place to which he had come in the previous week, when he was going to the island of Baneque. At first he did not dare to approach the land, because he thought that the sea broke heavily at that opening in the mountains. Finally he reached the Sea of Nuestra Señora, where there were many islands, and entered the harbour which is near the mouth of the entrance among the islands. And he says that if he had known of that harbour before and had not spent his time in examining the islands of the Sea of Nuestra Señora, [61] it would not have been necessary for him to go back, although he says that he felt that the time was well spent, since he had visited the said islands. So, having come to land, he sent the boat and sounded the harbour, and found a very good bottom, at six fathoms' depth and sometimes as much as twenty, and clean, sandy everywhere. He entered it, steering to the south-west, and afterwards going to the west, the flat island lying to the north. This island, with another near it, forms a bay in which all the ships of Spain could lie and could be safe from all winds without anchors. And this entrance on the south-east side, which is made steering south-south-west, has a way out to the west, very deep and very wide, so that it is possible to pass between the islands if one knows them, as it is the direct course along their shores for any one who comes from the open sea to the north. The islands lie at the foot of a big mountain, which stretches away from east to west and which is of great length and loftier and longer than any other on this coast, where there are innumerable mountains. Seaward, a reef extends the whole length of the said mountain, like a bar, which reaches as far as the entrance;

all this is on the south-eastern side. On the side of the flat island there
is also a reef, although it is small, and so between the two there is a
wide space and much depth of water, as has been said. Immediately
at the entrance, on the south-eastern side, within the same harbour,
they saw a large and very lovely river, and of greater volume than
those which they had hitherto seen, and the water was fresh as far as
the sea. At the entrance, it has a bar, but afterwards, within, it is very
deep, eight and nine fathoms. It is all surrounded by palms and many
trees, like the others.

SUNDAY, NOVEMBER 25th / Before sunrise, he entered the boat and
went to examine a cape or point of land to the south-east of the flat
island, a matter of a league and a half, because it seemed to him that
there should be a good river there. Directly at the beginning of the
cape, on the south-eastern side, having gone two crossbow shots, he
saw a large stream of very fine water flowing; it came down from
the mountain and made a great noise. He went to the river and saw
some stones shining in it, on which were some veins of the colour
of gold, and he remembered that in the river Tagus, at the mouth
of it, near the sea, gold is found, and it seemed to him to be certain
that there must be gold here, and he ordered some of those stones to
be collected to take them to the Sovereigns. While they were there,
the ships' boys shouted that they saw pines. He looked towards the
mountain and saw them, so tall and wonderful that he could not
overstate their height and straightness, like spindles, thick and slender.
From these he realised that ships could be built, and a vast quantity
of planks secured and masts for the largest ships in Spain. He saw
oaks and strawberry trees, and a good river, and means for constructing
saw-mills. The land and the breezes were more temperate than any
so far, owing to the height and beauty of the mountain ranges. He
saw on the beach many other stones, the colour of iron, and others
which some said came from silver mines. All these were brought down
by the river. There he secured a yard and a mast for the mizzen of
the caravel *Niña*. He reached the mouth of the river and entered a
creek, at the foot of that cape, on the south-east, very deep and large,
in which a hundred ships could lie, with no cables or anchors. The

A wonderous tree with three trunks; in Ramusio's *Navigationi et Viaggi*, 1606.

harbour was such that eyes never saw another like it; the mountains were very lofty and from them descend many very fine streams; all the high ground was full of pines, and everywhere were very diverse and very lovely groves of trees. Two or three other rivers lay behind.

He praises all this very highly to the Sovereigns, and declares that he felt inestimable pleasure and delight at seeing it, and especially the pines, because here could be built as many ships as might be wished, bringing out the materials, except timber and pitch, of which there would be an abundance there. And he affirms that he has not praised it to the hundredth part of that which might be said, and that it pleased Our Lord always to show him something better, and that continually in his discoveries up to then he had gone from good to better, as well in the matter of the lands and trees, herbs, fruit and flowers, as in that of the people, and always in a different manner, and as this was the case in one place, so it was in the next. The same was true of the ports and waters, and finally he says that if he who has seen it feels so great wonder, how much more wonderful will it be to one who hears of it, and that no one will be able to believe it if he has not seen it.

MONDAY, NOVEMBER 26th / At sunrise, they weighed anchor from the harbour of Santa Catalina, where he was within the flat island, and he steered along the coast, with little wind from the south-west, in the direction of Cape el Pico, which was to the south-east.[62] He reached the cape in the evening, because the wind dropped, and when he had arrived there, he saw to the south-east by east, another cape, which was sixty miles from him; and near there he saw another cape, which was south-east by south of the ship, and it seemed to him that it was twenty miles away, and to it he gave the name *Cape Campana.*[63] He was unable to reach it that day, because the wind again sank entirely. He may have made in the whole of that day thirty-two miles, which are eight leagues, in the course of which he noticed and marked nine well outlined harbours, which all the sailors marvelled at, and five large rivers, because he went continually near the shore, in order to see everything well. All that land has very high mountains, very lovely, and not dry or rocky, but all accessible, and very beautiful valleys. The valleys, as well as the mountains, were full of lofty and leafy trees, so that it was bliss to see them, and it seemed that there were many pines. And also behind Cape el Pico, to the south-east, there are two islets, each one of which is about two leagues in circumference, and within them three marvellous harbours and two large rivers. On all this coast he saw no inhabited place from the sea; there may have been some, and there were indications that this was so, because wherever they landed they found signs that there had been people and many fires. He considered that the land which he saw to-day to the south-east of Cape Campana was the island which the Indians called Bohio; this seemed to be so, because the cape is apart from that land. All the people who have been found up to this time have, he says, the very greatest fear of those of Caniba or Canima, and they

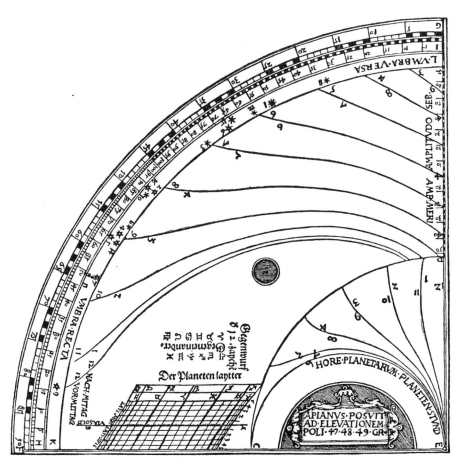

Apian's quadrant; in *Quadrans astronomicus*, 1532.

say that they live in this island of Bohio, which must be very large, as it appears, and he believes that those of Caniba take these people, since they are very cowardly and know nothing of arms, from their lands and houses. It seems to him that for this reason those Indians, whom he has with him, are not accustomed to settle on the coast of the sea, because their land is near Caniba. He says that when they saw that he was going in the direction of that land, they were speechless, fearing that they would be eaten, and he could not calm their terror; and they said that the people there had only one eye and the face of a dog. The admiral believed that they were lying, and he thought that they must be under the dominion of the Grand Khan who captured them.

TUESDAY, NOVEMBER 27th / Yesterday, at sunset, he arrived near a cape which he called Campana, and as the sky was clear and the wind slight, he did not wish to go to land to anchor, although to the leeward he had five or six marvellous harbours. Because he had delayed more than he had intended, owing to the desire which he had and the pleasure which he derived from seeing and wondering at the beauty and freshness of those lands, wherever he approached them, and in order not to delay the execution of his projects, for these reasons he remained that night beating about and standing off until day. As the drift and currents had carried him during that night more than five or six leagues to the south-east, beyond the point where he had been when night fell, and where the land of Campana had come in sight, and as beyond that cape a big opening appeared, which seemed to part one land from another and make as it were an island in the midst, he decided to go back with the wind south-west, and he came to the place where the opening had appeared. And he found that it was only a large bay, and at the end of it, on the south-east side, there was a cape, on which there was a mountain, lofty and square, which seemed to be an island.[64] The wind veered to the north, and he again turned to a south-easterly course, in order to run along the coast and to discover all that was there. Presently he saw at the foot of that Cape Campana a marvellous harbour and a large river; and a quarter of a league from there another river; and half a league from there another river; and a further half-

league on another river; and a league from there another river; and
another league from there another river; and another quarter of a
league from there another river; and another league from there another
large river, from which to Cape Campana was some twenty miles, and
they were to the south-east of him. Most of these rivers had large
entrances, wide and clear, with wonderful harbours for the very largest
ships, without bars of sand or rocks, or reefs. Coming so along the
coast, on the south-east, from the last-named river, he found a large
village, the largest that he had found up to this time, and he saw an
infinite number of people come to the seashore, shouting loudly, all
naked, with their spears in their hands. He wished to have speech with
them, and lowered the sails, and anchored, and sent the boats of the
ship and of the caravel, in an ordered manner, that they should do no
damage to the Indians and should receive none, commanding them
to give them some trifles from their articles of barter. The Indians made
a show of not allowing them to come ashore and of resisting them, and
then seeing that the boats came nearer to the shore and that they were
not afraid, they drew off from near the sea. And believing that, if two
or three men landed from the boats, they would not be frightened,
three Christians went on shore, telling them in their own language
that they should not fear, for they knew something of it from intercourse with those whom they had with them. Eventually the Indians
all took to flight, neither large nor small remaining. The three Christians went to the houses, which are of straw and of the form of the
others which they had seen, and they did not find anyone or anything
in any one of them. They returned to the ships and they hoisted sail at
midday to go to a beautiful cape which lay to the east, at a distance of
some eight leagues. Having gone half a league through the same bay,
the admiral saw toward the south a very remarkable harbour, and on
the south-east some marvellously beautiful lands, as it were a hilly tract
of land in the midst of these mountains, and much smoke and large
villages appeared among them, and the lands seemed to be very cultivated. Accordingly, he determined to run into this harbour and to
make an attempt to have speech or dealings with them. The harbour
was such that if he had praised the other harbours, he says that he
praised this the most, with its lands and temperate climate and its

surroundings and populousness. He says wonders of the beauty of the land and of the woods, where there are pines and palms, and of the great plain, which, although it is not entirely flat and stretches away to the south-south-east, but is undulated with smooth and low elevations, is the most lovely thing in the world, and through it flow many streams of water, which come down from these mountains. After the ship had been brought to anchor, the admiral jumped into the boat to take soundings in the harbour, which is like a bowl. When he was opposite the entrance to the south, he found the mouth of a river, which was wide enough for a galley to enter it, and of such a nature that it was invisible until it was reached. Entering it a boat's length, he found five and eight fathoms' depth of water. Proceeding by it, it was a marvellous thing to see the trees and the verdure and the very clear water and the birds, and its attractiveness, so that, as he says, he felt that he did not wish to leave it. He went on, telling the men whom he had in his company that, in order to give an account to the Sovereigns of the things which they had seen, a thousand tongues would not suffice for the telling nor his hand to write it, for it seemed to him that he was enchanted. He wished that many other persons, prudent and creditable, could see it, he says, being certain that they would not praise it less than he does. Here the admiral continues in these words: "How great will be the benefit which can be derived from this land, I do not write. It is certain, Sovereign Princes, that where there are such lands, there must be innumerable things of value, but I do not delay in any harbour, because I wish to see as many lands as I can, in order to give an account of them to Your Highnesses, and moreover I do not know the language, and the people of these lands do not understand me, nor do I or anyone I have with me understand them. These Indians also, whom I carry with me, I often misunderstand, taking one thing for the contrary, and I have no great confidence in them, because many times they have attempted to escape. But now, please Our Lord, I will see as much as I can, and little by little I shall come to understand and know, and I will cause persons of my household to learn this language, for I see that all, so far, have one language. And afterwards the benefits will be known, and an effort will be made to make all these peoples Christian, for that will be easily achieved, since they have no

A plant found in the New World; in Oviedo's *La hystoria generale de las Indias*, 1547.

creed and are not idolaters. And Your Highnesses will command that in these parts a city and fortress be established, and these lands will be converted. And I certify to Your Highnesses that nowhere under the sun do I think that there can be found lands superior in fertility, in moderation of cold and heat, in abundance of good and healthy water, and the rivers are not like those of Guinea, which are all pestilential. For, praise be to Our Lord, up to the present among all my people I have not had one who has had a headache or who has been in bed from illness, except one old man through pain from gravel, from which he has suffered all his life, and he was speedily well at the end of two days. This I say is the case in all the three vessels. So may it please God that Your Highnesses send here or that there come here learned men, and they will then see the truth of all. And since above I have spoken of the situation for a town and fortress on the river Mares, on account of the good harbour and of the surrounding district, it is certain that what I said is true, but it has no comparison with this place, nor has the Sea of Nuestra Señora. For here inland there must be great centres of population and innumerable people and things of great value, so that

I declare that here and in all else that I have discovered and which I have hopes of discovering before I go to Castile, all Christendom will find trade, and more especially Spain, to which all must be subject. And I say that Your Highnesses must not allow any stranger, except Catholic Christians, to trade here or set foot here, for this was the alpha and omega of the enterprise, that it should be for the increase and glory of the Christian religion and that no one should come to these parts who was not a good Christian." All these are his own words. There he went up the river and found some branches of the river, and going round the harbour he found that at the mouth of the river were some very lovely groves, like a very delectable orchard, and there he found a boat or canoe made of a single piece of wood, as large as a fusta of twelve seats,⁶⁶ very lovely; it was beached under a boat-house or shed made of timber and covered with large palm leaves, in such a way that neither the sun nor the rain could injure it. And he says that there was a suitable place for building a town or city and fortress, on account of the good harbour, good water, good land, good surroundings and abundance of wood.

WEDNESDAY, NOVEMBER 28th / He remained in that harbour that day, because it rained and was very cloudy, although he could have run all along the coast before the wind, which was south-west and would have been astern. But because he would not have been able to see the land well and because, not knowing it, it is dangerous for ships, he did not set out. The people from the ships landed to wash their clothes. Some of them went a certain distance inland; they found large villages and the houses empty, because all had fled. They returned down another river, larger than that in which they were harboured.

THURSDAY, NOVEMBER 29th / As it rained and the sky was accordingly overcast, he did not set out yesterday. Some of the Christians went to another village, near the north-western side, and in the houses they found no one and nothing. On the way they came up with an old man who was unable to run away from them. They took him and told him that they did not wish to hurt him, and gave him some trifling articles of barter, and let him go. The admiral would have liked to have seen him, in order to clothe him and have speech with him, because the

Indians at work; in Oviedo's *La hystoria generale de las Indias*, 1547.

felicity of that land and its suitability for the formation of a settlement greatly contented him; and he judged that there must be large centres of population. In one house they found a lump of wax which he brought to the Sovereigns, and he says that where there is wax, there must also be a thousand other good things. The sailors also found in one house a man's head in a small basket, covered with another basket, and hanging to a post of the house. They found another of the same kind in another village. The admiral believed that they must be the heads of some principal ancestors, because those houses were of a kind so that many persons find shelter in one house, and they could only be relations, descendants of one common ancestor.

FRIDAY, NOVEMBER 30th / He was not able to set out because the wind was east, very contrary to his course. He sent eight well-armed men, and two Indians with them, from among those whom he carried with him, to visit some villages inland and have speech. They reached many houses, and they found no person or thing, for they had all fled. They saw four youths who were digging in their fields. When they saw the Christians, they turned at once in flight, and the Christians could not overtake them. They went, he says, a considerable distance; they saw many villages and very fertile land and all cultivated, and large streams of water. Near one they saw a boat or canoe, ninety-five palms long, made of a single piece of wood, very beautiful, and in which a hundred and fifty persons could be contained and navigate.

SATURDAY, DECEMBER 1st / He again did not set out because of the contrary wind and because it rained heavily. He set up a great cross on some bare rocks at the entrance of that harbour, which, I believe, he called *Puerto Santo*. The point is that which is on the south-eastern side at the entrance of the harbour, and whoever wishes to enter this harbour must go rather to the point which is on the north-western side than to that on the south-east, because, although at the foot of both points, near the rock, there is a depth of twelve fathoms and very clear water, yet at the entrance of the harbour, near the south-eastern point, there is shoal above the surface of the water. This is far enough from the point for it to be possible to pass between if there is need, for between the end of the shoal and the cape there is everywhere a depth of twelve and fifteen fathoms. At the entrance, the course is to south-west.

SUNDAY, DECEMBER 2nd / The wind was still contrary and he could not leave. He says that every night there is a land breeze, and that however many ships might be there, they need have no fear of any storm whatsoever since it could not reach the ships inside, on account of a shoal which is at the entrance of the harbour, etc. He says that at the mouth of that river a ship's boy found some stones which seemed to bear gold. He brought them to show to the Sovereigns. He says that there are large rivers at a lombard shot from there.

MONDAY, DECEMBER 3rd / Owing to the fact that the weather was always unsuitable, he did not leave that harbour, and he decided to go to see a very lovely cape, a quarter of a league from the harbour, to the south-east. He went with the boats and some armed men. At the foot of the cape there was the mouth of a good river; he steered south-east to enter it, and it was a hundred paces wide; it was a fathom deep at the entrance or mouth, but within it was twelve fathoms, five, four and two, and as many ships as there are in Spain could lie there. And leaving a branch of that river, he went to the south-east and found a creek, in which he saw five very large boats, which the Indians call "canoes," like fustas, very beautiful and carved, so that he says that it was a delight to see them. At the foot of the mountain, he saw that it was everywhere cultivated. They went under very thick trees, and

Types of caravels; in Pedro Medina's *Arte De Navegar*, 1545.

going along the way which led to them, they came upon a boat-house,
very well arranged and roofed, so that neither sun nor water could do
damage, and in it there was another canoe, made of a single piece of
timber like the others, of the size of a fusta of seventeen benches, and

it was a pleasure to see its workmanship and beauty. He ascended a
mountain and found its top all level and sown with pumpkins and other
products of the land, so that it was glorious to behold, and in the
middle of it there was a large village. He came suddenly upon the
people of the village, and as soon as they saw them, men and women
took to flight. The Indian, one of those whom he carried with him,
who accompanied him, reassured them, saying that they need not fear,
for they were good people. The admiral caused them to be given hawks'
bells and brass rings, and small green and yellow glass beads, with
which they were well content, having seen that they had no gold and
nothing else of value, and that he might well leave them in peace, and
that all the neighbourhood was inhabited, the others having fled
from fear.   And the admiral assures the Sovereigns that ten men
would make ten thousand take to flight; so cowardly and fearful are
they, that they do not bear arms, except some spears, at the end of
which there is a sharp stick, hardened in the fire. He decided to return.
He says that with some cleverness he took the spears from them, bar-
tering for them, so that they gave them all up. Returning to the place
where they had left the boats, he sent some Christians to the place to
which they had ascended, because it had seemed to him that he had
seen a large apiary. Before those whom he had sent came back, many
Indians gathered and came to the boats where the admiral had now
collected all his men again. One of them went forward into the river
near the stern of the boat and made a great oration, which the admiral
did not understand, except that the other Indians from time to time
raised their hands to heaven and shouted loudly. The admiral thought
that they were reassuring him and that they were pleased with his
coming, but he saw the Indian, whom he carried with him, change his
expression and become as yellow as wax and tremble greatly, saying by
signs that the admiral should leave the river because they wished to kill
him. And he went up to a Christian who had a loaded crossbow and
pointed this out to the Indians, and the admiral gathered that he was
telling them that they would kill them all because that crossbow carried far and slew. He also took a sword and drew it from its sheath,
exhibiting it and saying the same. When they heard this, they all took
to flight, the above-mentioned Indian still remaining trembling from

cowardice and faint-heartedness; and he was a man of good stature and strong. The admiral would not leave the river until he had himself rowed to the shore where they were: they were many, all stained red and naked as their mothers bore them, and some of them had feathers on their heads and other plumes, and all had handfuls of darts. "I went towards them and gave them some mouthfuls of bread and asked them for the darts; and I gave to some a hawk's bell, to others a small brass ring, to others some small beads, with the result that they were all pacified and they all came to the boats, and they gave whatever they had for what was given to them, whatever it might be. The sailors had killed a tortoise and the shell was in pieces in the boat, and the ships' boys gave a piece of it as large as a finger nail, and the Indians gave them a handful of darts. They are people like the others whom I have found," says the admiral, "and they have the same belief and think that we have come from heaven. Whatever they have they give at once for anything that may be given to them, without saying

A fish called 'manati'; in Oviedo's *La hystoria general de las Indias*, 1547.

that it is little, and I believe that they would do so with spices and gold, if they had any. I saw a beautiful house, not very large, and with two entrances, for so have they all, and I entered it, and I saw a wonderful arrangement like rooms, made in a certain manner that I know not how to describe, and hanging from the ceiling of it were shells and other things. I thought that it was a temple and called them, and I asked them by signs if they offered prayer in it; they said, No. One of them went up above and gave me everything that was there, and I took some of it."

TUESDAY, DECEMBER 4th / He set sail with a light wind and left that harbour, which he named Puerto Santo. At two leagues' distance he saw a good river, of which he spoke yesterday. He went along the coast and all the land ran past the said cape, to the east-south-east and west-north-west, as far as Cape Lindo,[67] which is to the east by south of Cape del Monte, and it is five leagues from one to the other. A league and a half from Cape del Monte there is a large river, somewhat narrow. It seemed to have a good entrance and to be very deep, and from there at a distance of three-quarters of a league he saw another very large river, which must come from a great distance. At the mouth it is a good hundred paces wide, and there is no bar at it, and at the mouth there are eight fathoms of water and the entrance is good, because he sent to see and to take soundings from the boat. The fresh water comes down to the sea, and the river is one of the most considerable that he has found, and there must be large villages on it. After Cape Lindo there is a great bay, which might be a good passage to the east-north-east and south-east and south-south-west.[68]

WEDNESDAY, DECEMBER 5th / All this night he beat about off Cape Lindo, where he was at nightfall, in order to examine the land which ran to the east. At sunrise, he saw another cape two leagues and a half to the east;[69] having passed that, he saw that the coast trended to the south and inclined to the south-west, and presently he saw a very lovely and lofty cape on the said course, and the distance between the two was seven leagues. He would have liked to go there, but he abandoned the idea, because he wished to go to the island of Baneque, which lay to the north-east, according to what the Indians whom he had with him said. Yet he could not go to Baneque either, for the wind which he had was north-east. As he so proceeded, he looked to the south-east and saw land, and it was a very large island, of which, as he says, he had already received information from the Indians, who called it "Bohio," that it was populous. Of these people, he says that those of Cuba or Juana and all these other islands are much afraid, because they say that they eat men. The Indians told him by signs other very marvellous things, but the admiral says that he did not believe them, but that the people of that island of Bohio must be more astute and have greater intelligence than they to capture them, because these men are very faint-hearted. So, as the wind was north-east northerly, he decided to leave Cuba or Juana, which up to then he had regarded as being the mainland owing to its extent, for he had gone fully a hundred and twenty leagues along one side of it. And he departed to the south-east by east. Since the land which he had seen trended towards the south-east, this gave protection, because the wind was constantly changing from the north to the north-east and from there to the east and south-east. The wind changed greatly, and he carried all sail, the sea being smooth and the current favouring him, with the result that, up to the first hour after midday, from the morning, he made eight miles an hour, and that time was six hours, but not quite so, because he says that there the nights are about fifteen hours long. Afterwards he went ten miles an hour. So up to sunset he made some eighty-eight miles, which are twenty-two leagues, always to the south-east. And as night was falling, he ordered the caravel *Niña*, as she was fast, to go forward in order to examine the harbour before dark. Having arrived at the mouth of the harbour, which was like the bay of Cadiz, and as it was already night, she sent her boat, carrying a light, to take soundings in the harbour. Before the admiral came to where the caravel was lying to and waiting for the boat to make signals that she should enter the harbour, the light in the boat was extinguished. The caravel, as she saw no light, ran out and showed a light to the admiral, and when he came up with her, they told him what had occurred. Just at this point, those in the boat lit another light. The caravel went to it, and the admiral could not and remained all that night, beating about.

THURSDAY, DECEMBER 6th / At dawn, he found himself four leagues from the harbour; he named it *Puerto Maria*.[70] He saw a lovely cape to the south by west, which he named *Cape Estrella*,[71] and it seemed to him that it was the last land of this island towards the south, and that the admiral was distant from it twenty-eight miles. Another land appeared, like an island of small size, toward the east, at a distance of about forty miles. To the east by south, at a distance of some fifty-four miles, there lay another very beautiful and well-shaped cape, which he named *Cape Elephant*. Another cape lay east-south-east of him, and this he named *Cape Cinquin*;[72] it was some twenty-eight miles away. South-east, easterly, at a distance of some twenty miles from him, there lay a great cutting or opening or arm of the sea, which seemed to be a river; it seemed that there was a wide inlet between Cape Elephant and Cape Cinquin, and some of the sailors said that it was a division of the island; that he named *Isla de la Tortuga*.[73] That large island seemed to be very high land, not fenced in by mountains, but level like lovely farmland, and it seemed to be entirely cultivated or a great part of it, and the crops looked like wheat does in May in the fields of Cordoba. Many fires were seen that night, and by day much smoke as if from lookouts, which seemed to be designed to guard against some people with whom they were at war. All the coast of this land trends to the east. At the hour of vespers he entered the said harbour and named it *Puerto de San Nicolas*, in honour of St. Nicholas, because it was his feast; and at its entrance he wondered at its beauty and goodness, and although he had greatly praised the harbours of Cuba, yet he says that beyond doubt this is not less to be praised but rather surpasses them, and there is none like it. At the mouth and entrance it is a league and a half wide, and one should steer to the south-south-east, although owing to its great breadth one can steer in whatever direction one wishes. In this way he went two leagues to the south-south-east. At its entrance, to the southward, it forms a kind of promontory, and from there it extends about the same distance to the end, where there is a very lovely beach and a field of trees of a thousand kinds, all laden with fruit, which the admiral believed to be spices and nutmegs, but they were not ripe and he did not recognise them. In the centre of the beach there is a river. The depth of this harbour is marvellous, since at a

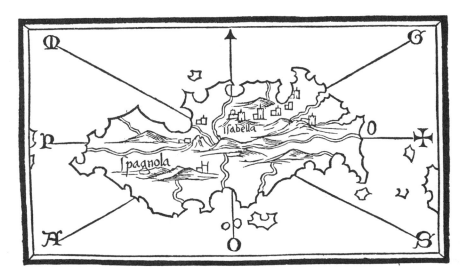

The islands of Española and Isabella; in Bordone's *Isolario*, 1528.

distance of the length of a . . . from the land it could not be sounded
or any bottom reached at a depth of forty fathoms, and within that
distance it has a depth of fifteen fathoms and is very clear. And so
the whole harbour within each point at a distance of five feet from
land is fifteen fathoms deep and free from rocks. In the same way
all this coast has very deep and clear water, so that there does not
seem to be a single shoal, and at its foot, at a distance of a boat's oar
from land, there are five fathoms. Beyond the end of the harbour,
going towards the south-south-east, and within it, a thousand carracks
could beat about; an arm of the harbour extends to the north-east,
running into the land a full half-league, and everywhere of the same
breadth as if it had been measured with a tape. It lay in such a manner
that, being in that arm which was twenty-five paces wide, the mouth
of the main entrance was invisible, as if it were an enclosed harbour.
The depth of this arm from its beginning to its end is eleven fathoms,
and it is everywhere *basa* or clean sand, and at the shore and at a
distance at which the gunwales could be laid against the grass, it has
eight fathoms' depth. All the harbour is very breezy and unsheltered,
bare of trees. All this island seems to be more rocky than any that he

had found hitherto; the trees are smaller and many of them are of the same kind as in Spain, such as oaks and strawberry trees and others, and the same is true of the plants. The land is very high and is all open country or clear; the air is very good and he had not found such cold as here, although it could hardly be described as cold, except in comparison with the other lands. Opposite the harbour there was a beautiful fertile plain and in the middle of it the river already mentioned, and he says that in this neighbourhood there must be large centres of population, judging from the appearance of the canoes in which they navigate, which were very numerous and as large as a fusta of fifteen benches. All the Indians took to flight and fled when they saw the ships. Those whom he carried with him from the smaller islands were very anxious to go to their own land, and their idea was, says the admiral, that when he left that place, he would take them to their homes, and they already regarded it as suspicious, that he was not taking the route to their home. On this account he says that he did not believe what they told him, nor did he understand them well or they him, and he says that they had the greatest fear in the world of the people of that island. To have speech with the people of that island, he would have been obliged to remain thus for some days in that harbour; but he did not do this, in order that he might discover much land, and because he was doubtful whether the fair weather would continue. He hoped in Our Lord that the Indians, whom he had with him, would learn his language and he theirs, and afterwards he would return and have speech with those people, and with God's help, as he says, he should have some good trade in gold before his return.

FRIDAY, DECEMBER 7th / At the passing of the quarter of dawn, he set sail and left the harbour of St. Nicholas. He navigated with the wind south-west two leagues to the north-east, as far as a cape which the beach makes; a promontory lay to his south-east and Cape Estrella to the south-west, at a distance of twenty-four miles from the admiral. Thence he navigated along the coast eastward, as far as Cape Cinquin, which was some forty-eight miles. In actual fact twenty were to the east by north. All that coast is very high land and there is great depth

of water; close to the shore it is twenty and thirty fathoms, and it is
so deep that at about a lombard's shot from land, bottom could not
be reached. All this the admiral proved that day, much to his delight,
as he went along the coast with a south-west wind. The promontory,
mentioned above, extends, he says, within a lombard shot of the
harbour of St. Nicholas, so that if that distance were pierced or
cut through, an island would be formed; the part cut off would have
a circumference of three to four miles.[74] All that land is very high; it
has no large trees, but only oaks and strawberry trees, like, he says,
the land of Castile. Before he reached Cape Cinquin, at a distance of
two leagues, he found a small opening, like a ravine in a mountain,
through which he caught sight of a very large valley, and he saw that
it was all apparently sown with barley, and he thought that there must
be big villages in that valley. At its sides there rose great and very
lofty mountains. When he reached Cape Cinquin, the head of the
island of Tortuga lay to the north-east at a distance of about thirty-
two miles, and near this Cape Cinquin, at a lombard shot, there is a
rock in the sea which rises high and can thus be easily seen. The
admiral being off the said cape, Cape Elephant lay to the east by south,
and it was some seventy miles to it. All the land was very high. At
the end of six leagues[75] he found a great bay and saw inland large
valleys and cultivated fields and very high mountains, all resembling
Castile. Eight miles from there he found a very deep river, but it was
narrow, although it would have been possible to enter it in a carrack;
the mouth was all clear, without a bar or shoals. Sixteen miles from
there he found a very wide harbour, very deep, so that he could not
find bottom at the entrance or at three paces from the shore, except
at fifteen fathoms, and it ran inland a quarter of a league. And although it was still early, about an hour after midday, and the wind was
astern and fresh, since the sky showed that it was about to rain
heavily, and was very overcast, which indicates danger even off a
shore which is known and much more off one which is not known,
he decided to enter the harbour, which he called *Puerto de la Concepción*.[76] He made land in a river which is not very large and is at the
head of the harbour; it flows through some plains and fields, the
beauty of which was a wonder to see. He took nets to fish, and before

he reached the shore a skate, like those of Spain itself, jumped into the boat. Up to that time he had seen no fish which seemed to be like those of Castile. The sailors went fishing and caught some, as well as soles and other fish like those of Castile. He went a short distance into that country, which is all cultivated, and he heard the nightingales [77] and other birds singing, like those of Castile. They saw five men, who would not wait but took to flight. He found myrtle, and other trees and plants, which, no less than the land and mountains, recalled Castile.

SATURDAY, DECEMBER 8th / There in that harbour they had heavy rain, with a very strong north wind. The harbour is sheltered from all winds, except the north, and that can do no damage, because the surf is heavy and prevents the ships from dragging at their anchors or the water of the river from being disturbed. After midnight, the wind changed to the north-east and then to the east, from which winds that harbour is well protected by the island of Tortuga, which lies opposite to it at a distance of thirty-six miles.

SUNDAY, DECEMBER 9th / This day it rained and the weather became wintry like October in Castile. He had seen no dwelling except a very beautiful house on the harbour of St. Nicholas, which was better made than those in the other places which he had visited. The island is very large and the admiral says that it would not be an overestimate to say that it has a circumference of two hundred leagues. He had observed that it is all well cultivated. He believed that the villages must be at a distance from the sea and that from them they saw when he arrived and so all took to flight, carrying with them all that they had and lighting warning fires, like soldiers. At its entrance this harbour is a thousand paces wide, which are a quarter of a league; there is in it no bar or shoal, but on the contrary bottom can hardly be found close to land by the seashore. Within it extends for three thousand paces; it is all clear and with a sandy bottom, so that any ship could anchor in it without fear and enter without hesitation. At its end there are two river mouths; they bring down little water. Opposite its end there are some plains, the loveliest in the world, and as fit for sowing as

The islands discovered by Columbus; in the illustrated edition of the Columbus letter, 1493.

the lands of Castile, and indeed these are superior. For this reason, he named the island *Española*.

MONDAY, DECEMBER 10th / It blew strongly from the north-east, which caused the anchors to drag about half a cable's length. At this the admiral was surprised, and he thought that it was because the anchors were near land and the wind blew towards it. And seeing that the wind was contrary for the course which he wished to follow, he sent six men, well equipped with arms, on land, to go two or three leagues inland, in order to discover if they could have speech. They went and returned, having found neither men nor houses. They found, however, some huts and very wide roads, and places where many people had made fires. They saw the best lands in the world, and they found many mastic trees and brought some of it, and they said there was much, but it was not yet the time for gathering it, because it did not form gum.

TUESDAY, DECEMBER 11th / He did not set out owing to the wind which was still east and north-east. Opposite that port, as has been said, is the island of Tortuga, and it seems to be a large island and its coast runs almost as does that of Española, and from the one to the other it was, at the most, ten leagues, that is to say, from Cape Cinquin to the head of Tortuga, which is to the north of Española. Afterwards its coast runs to the south. He says that he was anxious to examine the strait between these two islands, in order to view the island of Española, which is the loveliest thing in the world and because, according to the Indians whom he had brought there, that was the direction of the island of Baneque. They told him that this island was very great and had very large mountains and rivers and valleys, and they said that the island of Bohio was larger than that of Juana, which they call Cuba, and that it is not surrounded with water. It appears that they meant that it was mainland and that it is here, behind this Española, which they call Caritaba, and that it is of infinite extent, and it appears likely that they are harassed by an intelligent race, all these islands living in great fear of those of Caniba. "And so I repeat what I have said on other occasions," he says, "the Caniba are nothing else than the people of the Grand Khan, who must be very near here

Trees which produce gourds; in Benzoni's *Historia del Mondo Nuovo*, 1563.

and possess ships, and they must come to take them captive, and as the prisoners do not return, they believe that they have been eaten. Every day we understand these Indians better and they us, although many times there has been misunderstanding," says the admiral. He sent men ashore; they found much mastic which was not yet gummy. He says that the rains must do this, and that in Chios they gather it in March, and that in those lands, as they are so temperate, they would gather it in January. They caught many fish, like those of Castile—dace, salmon, hake, dory, pampano, mullet, congers, shrimps; and they saw sardines. They found much aloe.

WEDNESDAY, DECEMBER 12th / He did not set out on this day, for the reason already given of the contrary wind. He set up a great cross at the entrance of the harbour, on the western side, on a very conspicuous height, "As a sign," he says, "that Your Highnesses hold this land as your own, and especially as an emblem of Jesus Christ, Our Lord, and to the honour of Christendom." When this had been set up, three sailors went up the mountain to see the trees and plants, and they saw a great crowd of people, all naked like those found before. They called to them and went towards them, but the Indians took to flight. Eventually they took a woman, as they could not take any more, "For I had given orders," he says, "that they should take some, treat them well and make them lose their fear, that some gain might be made, since, considering the beauty of the land, it could not be but that there was gain to be got." So they brought the woman, a very young and lovely girl, to the ship, and she spoke to those Indians, for they all had the same language. The admiral caused her to be clothed and gave her glass beads and hawks' bells and brass rings, and sent her back to land very honourably, according to his custom. He sent some of the ship's company with her and three of the Indians, whom he had with him, to talk to those people. The sailors who went in the boat told the admiral that when they brought her to land, she did not wish to leave the ship, but to stay with the other Indian women, whom he had taken at Puerto de Mares in the island of Juana or Cuba. All the Indians who were with that Indian woman came, he says, in a canoe, which is for them a caravel, in which they navigate everywhere, and when they appeared at the entrance of the harbour and saw the ships, they turned back and left the canoe in some place there, and went towards their village. She showed them the situation of this village. This woman had a small piece of gold in her nose, which was an indication that there was gold in that island.

THURSDAY, DECEMBER 13th / The three men, whom the admiral had sent with the woman, returned at three o'clock at night, and they had not gone with her as far as the village, because it seemed to be far or because they were afraid. They said that on the next day many people would come to the ships, since they could only be reassured by the news which the woman would give them. The admiral longed to know whether there was anything of value in that land and to have some speech with those people, because the land was so lovely and

The Indian method of making bread; in Benzoni's *Historia del Mondo Nuovo*, 1563.

fertile; and he also wished that they might become eager to serve the Sovereigns. For these reasons, he decided to send again to the village, trusting in the news that the Indian woman would have given that the Christians were good people, and for this purpose he selected nine men, well supplied with arms and fitted for such a business, and with them went an Indian, of those whom he carried with him. These men went to the village, which was four and a half leagues to the south-east. They found it in a very large valley, and it was abandoned, for, as soon as they perceived the Christians, all fled into the interior, leaving whatever they had. The village was of a thousand houses and of more than three thousand inhabitants. The Indian, whom the Christians took with them, ran after them, shouting, saying that they need not be afraid, for the Christians were not from Caniba, but rather came from heaven, and that they gave beautiful things to all whom they found. What he said so greatly impressed them that they were reassured, and more than two thousand of them came all together, and they all came to the Christians and placed their hands on their heads, which was a mark of great respect and friendship; yet they were all trembling until they had been greatly reassured. The Christians said that when at last they had lost their fear, they went to their houses, one and all, and each one of them brought to them what they had to eat, which is bread of "niamas,"[78] that is, of roots like large carrots which they grow, for they sow and grow and cultivate this in all these lands, and it is their mainstay of life. They make bread from these roots and boil and roast them, and they taste like chestnuts, so that no one eating them would believe that they are anything but chestnuts. They gave them bread and fish, and whatever they had. And as the Indians whom he had in the ship had understood that the admiral wished to have a parrot, it seems that the Indian who went with the Christians told them something of this, and so they brought them parrots and gave them as many as they asked, without wishing to have anything in return. They asked them not to go back that night, and then they would give them many other things which they had in the mountains. At the moment when all those people were with the Christians they saw a great array or crowd of people coming with the husband of the woman whom the admiral had treated with honour and sent back, and they brought her, riding on their shoulders, and they came to give thanks to the Christians for the honour which the admiral had shown her and the gifts given to her. The Christians told the admiral that all these people were more handsome and of better character than any of the others whom they had found up to that time, but the admiral says that he does not know how they could be of better character than the others, by which he means to imply that all those who had been found in the other islands were of very good character. As to their personal appearance, the Christians said that there was no comparison either for men or women and that they are fairer than the others; among them, they saw two young women as white as any that could be found in Spain. They said also, concerning the beauty of the lands which they saw, that the best lands in Castile for beauty and fertility could not be compared with these. And the admiral saw that this was so from those lands which he had visited and from those which he had before him, and they told him that these could not be compared with those of that valley, which the plain of Cordoba did not equal, the two being as different as day and night. They said that all those lands were cultivated, and that through the middle of that valley there flowed a river, very wide and great, which could water all the lands. All the trees were green and full of fruit, and the plants all flowering and very tall, the roads very wide and good, the breezes like those of Castile in April. The nightingale and other small birds were singing as they do in that month in Spain, and he says that it was the greatest delight in the world. At night some small birds sang sweetly, and many crickets and frogs were heard. The fish were as those of Spain; they saw much mastic and aloe and cotton trees. They found no gold, nor is this surprising in the very short while that they were there. Here the admiral tested the length of the day and night, and from sunset to sunrise was twenty half-hour glasses, although he says that there may have been some error, either because they were not turned quickly enough or because the sand did not all pass through. He also says that he found by the quadrant that he was thirty-four degrees from the equinoctial line.[79]

FRIDAY, DECEMBER 14th / He left that harbour of Concepción with a land breeze, and very soon it became calm, as had been the case every day that he had been there. Afterwards an east wind sprang up and he steered with it to the north-north-east; he reached the island of Tortuga and saw a point of it which he named *Punta Pierna*, which was to the east-north-east of the head of the island, at a distance of twelve miles. And from there he sighted another point which he called *Punta Lançada*, in the same direction to the north-east, at a distance of some sixteen miles. So from the head of the island of Tortuga as far as Punta Aguda it was some forty-four miles, which are eleven leagues, to the east-north-east. On that course there were some stretches of wide beach. This island of Tortuga is very high land, but not mountainous, and is very lovely and very populous, like the island of Española, and the whole land is so cultivated that it looks

like the plain of Cordoba. Seeing that the wind was contrary and that
he could not go to the island of Baneque, he decided to return to the
harbour of Concepción, whence he had set out, and he was unable to
make a river which is two leagues from the said harbour towards
the east.

SATURDAY, DECEMBER 15th / He again left the harbour of Concepción
on his voyage, but on leaving the harbour, the east wind blew strongly
against him and he steered towards Tortuga, which he reached. From
there he went about to examine that river which he had wished to
examine and reach yesterday and was unable to do. On this occasion
again he could not make it, although he anchored half a league to the
leeward, off a beach, a good and clear anchorage. Having secured his
ships, he went with the boats to examine the river and entered an arm
of the sea which is half a league short of it and was not a river mouth;
he turned back and found the mouth which was not even a fathom
deep and where there was a very strong current. He entered it with
the boats, to reach the villages which those whom he had sent the
day before yesterday had visited; he ordered the line to be thrown
ashore and the sailors, pulling at it, brought the boats two lombard
shots up, and it was impossible to go farther owing to the strength
of the current of the river. He saw some houses and the large
valley, where the villages lay, and he said that he had never seen anything more lovely, and through the middle of that valley flowed that
river. He saw people also at the entrance to the river, but they all took to
flight. He says further that those people must be greatly hunted, since
they live in such a state of terror, because when they arrived at any
point, immediately these people made smoke signals from lookouts
throughout the land, and this was more the case in this island of
Española and in that of Tortuga, which is also a large island, than
in the other islands which he had left behind. He called the valley
Valle del Paraiso, and the river *Guadalquivir*,[80] for he says that it flows
as strongly as the Guadalquivir by Cordoba, and on its edges or banks
there is a beach of very lovely stones and it is all accessible.

SUNDAY, DECEMBER 16th / At midnight, with a light land breeze, he
set sail to go out from that gulf, and coming from the coast of the

The Indian method of navigation; in Benzoni's *Historia del Mondo Nuovo*, 1563.

island of Española, sailing close-hauled, because presently at the hour of terce it blew from the east, and in mid-channel, he found a canoe with a solitary Indian in it. At this the admiral was amazed, wondering how he could keep above water, the wind being high. He had him and his canoe taken on board the ship, and to please him gave him glass beads, hawks' bells and brass rings, and carried him in the ship ashore at a village which was sixteen miles from there near the sea. There the admiral anchored and found good anchorage by the beach near the village, which seemed to have been recently established as all the houses were new. [81] The Indian at once went ashore in his canoe, and gave news of the admiral and of the Christians as being good people, although they already held them to be so on account of the experience of the others where the six Christians had gone. Presently there came more than five hundred men, and a little afterwards there came their king. All came down to the beach near the ships, for they were anchored very close to the shore. Then one by one, and many at a time, they came to the ship, bringing nothing with them, although some wore some grains of very fine gold on their ears or noses, which they immediately gave with great readiness. The admiral ordered honour to be done to all of them, and he says: "They are the best people in the world and beyond all the mildest, so that I have much hope in Our Lord that Your Highnesses will make them all Christians, and that they will be all yours, for I regard them as yours." He saw also that the king was on the beach and that they all showed him respect. The admiral sent him a present, which he received with much ceremony; he was a young man of some twenty-one years, and he had an old governor and other counsellors, who advised him and answered for him, and he himself said very few words. One of the Indians whom the admiral carried with him spoke to him and told him how the Christians came from heaven and that their journey was in search of gold and that it was their wish to go to the island of Baneque. He answered that it was well and that in the said island there was much gold, and to the alguacil of the admiral, who carried the present to him, he showed the route which should be taken and explained that in two days they could arrive there from this place, and if they had need of anything from his land, he would give it with very good will. This king and all the others went naked as their mothers had borne them, and so did the women, with no trace of shame. They are the most handsome men and women whom they had found up to then, so very fair that, if they were clothed and protected themselves from the sun and air, they would be almost as white as the people of Spain, for this land is very cool and the best that tongue can describe. It is very lofty and on the highest mountain oxen could plough and all could be made like the plains and valleys. In all Castile there is no land which could be compared to this for beauty and fertility; all this island and that of Tortuga is as cultivated as the plain of Cordoba. They have them sown with *ajes*, which are certain slips which they plant, and at the foot of them grow some roots like carrots, which serve as bread, and they grate them, knead

them and make bread of them. Afterwards they again plant the same
slip in another place and it again produces four or five of these
roots, which are very savoury and have the exact taste of chestnuts.
Those here are the largest and best that he had seen in any land, for
he also says that they are found in Guinea; these here were as thick as
a leg. He says of these people that they were all stout and valiant and
not feeble like the others whom he had previously found, and with
very pleasant voices; they have no creed. He says that the trees there
grew so luxuriantly that their leaves were no longer green but dark
coloured. It was a thing of wonder to behold those valleys and those
rivers and fair springs of water, and the lands suited for growing
bread, for raising stock of all kinds, of which they have none, for
gardens, and for everything in the world that a man could desire.
Afterwards, in the evening, the king came to the ship; the admiral
showed him due honour and caused him to be told that he came from
the Sovereigns of Castile who were the greatest princes in the world.
Neither the Indians whom the admiral carried with him, and who
were the interpreters, nor the king either, believed anything of this,
but they were convinced that they came from heaven and that the
realms of the Sovereigns of Castile were in heaven and not in this
world. They placed before the king things to eat from Castile, and
he ate a mouthful and afterwards gave it all to his counsellors and to
the governor and to the others whom he brought with him. "Your
Highnesses may believe that these lands are of such extent, good and
fertile, and especially those of this island of Española, that no one
knows how to describe them and no one can believe it, unless he has
seen it. And you may believe that this island and all the others are
as much your own as Castile, so that there is lacking here nothing
except a settlement and then to command them to do what you wish.
For I, with these people whom I carry with me, who are not many,
could go about all these islands without meeting opposition, for now
I have seen three of these sailors land alone, where there was a crowd
of Indians, and they have all fled, without any one wishing to harm
them. They have no arms and are all naked and without any knowledge of war, and very cowardly, so that a thousand of them would
not face three. And they are also fitted to be ruled and to be set to

work, to cultivate the land and to do all else that may be necessary, and you may build towns and teach them to go clothed and adopt our customs."

MONDAY, DECEMBER 17th / That night the wind blew strongly from the east-north-east; the sea was not very rough, because the island of Tortuga, which is opposite and forms a shelter, protected and guarded it. He was there in this way for that day. He sent the sailors fishing with nets; the Indians mixed freely with the Christians and brought them some arrows belonging to the Canibatos or the Cannibals, and they are made of the spikes of canes and are tipped with some small sticks, hardened in the fire and sharp, and they are very large. Two men showed them that some bits of flesh were missing from their bodies and gave them to understand that the Cannibals had bitten mouthfuls from them. The admiral did not believe this. He again sent some Christians to the village, and in exchange for some glass beads they secured some pieces of gold worked into a thin leaf. They saw one man, whom the admiral took for the governor of that province, whom they called "cacique," with a piece of gold leaf as large as the hand, and it seemed that he wished to exchange it. He went to his house and the others remained in the square, and he caused that piece to be broken into small pieces and exchanged it, bringing one small piece at a time. When there was none left, he said by signs that he had sent for more and that next day they would bring it. All these things, and the manner of them, and their customs and mildness and behaviour showed them to be a more alert and intelligent people than the others whom he had found up to that time. The admiral says: "In the afternoon there arrived a canoe from the island of Tortuga with quite forty men, and when it reached the beach, all the people of the village, which was near, sat down as a sign of peace, and almost all those in the canoe landed. The cacique alone arose, and with words which seemed to be threats, made them go back to the canoe, and threw them water and took stones from the beach and threw them into the water, and after that they all with great obedience settled down and embarked in the canoe. He then took a stone and placed it in the hand of my alguacil, whom I had sent to land with the secretary

The attire of an Indian woman; in Benzoni's *Historia del Mondo Nuovo*, 1563.

and others to see if they could bring back anything of value, for him to throw it, and the alguacil did not wish to throw it." In this way that cacique showed clearly that he favoured the admiral. Presently the canoe went away, and after it had gone, they told the admiral that in Tortuga there was more gold than in the island of Española, because it was nearer to Baneque. The admiral says that he does not believe that there are mines of gold either in that island of Española or in Tortuga, but that they bring it from Baneque and they bring little, because they have nothing to give for it. That land is so rich that there is no need for them to labour much to get themselves food and clothing, especially as they go naked. And the admiral believed that he was very near the source of the gold and that Our Lord would show him where it originated. He had information that from there to Baneque it was four days' journey, which would be some thirty or forty leagues, so that they could go there in one day of fair weather.

TUESDAY, DECEMBER 18th / All this day he remained anchored by that beach, because there was no wind, and also because the cacique had said that he would bring gold—not that the admiral set much store by the gold which he would bring, he says, because there were no mines there, but he would know better whence they brought it. Presently, when dawn came, he commanded the ship and the caravel to be decked with arms and banners for the festival which was the day of Santa Maria de la O, or commemoration of the Annunciation.[82] They fired many shots from the lombards, and the king of that island of Española, says the admiral, had started early from his house, which must have been five leagues away from there, as far as he could judge, and at the hour of terce came to that village, where there were already some whom the admiral had sent from the ship to see if the gold had come. They said that the king was on his way with more than two hundred men, that four men carried him in a litter, and that he was a young man, as has been said above. To-day, while the admiral was dining below the castle, he came to the ship with all his people. And the admiral says to the Sovereigns: "There is no doubt that Your Highnesses would think well of his estate and of the respect which all have for him, although they all go naked. As soon as he came on board the ship, he found that I was eating at the table below the stern castle, and, hurrying up, he came and seated himself beside me, and he would not allow me to go to meet him or to rise from table, but wished me to continue my meal. I thought that he would be pleased to eat of our viands; I immediately commanded things to be brought for him to eat. And when he came in below the castle, he made signs with his hand that all his men should remain outside, and they did so with the greatest readiness and respect in the world, and they all seated themselves on the deck, except two men of mature age, whom I think were his counsellors and one his governor, who came and sat at his feet. And of the viands which I placed before him, he took of each kind as much as may be taken to taste it and afterwards at once sent the rest to his people, and they all ate of them. So also he did with

Cannibals; detail of an engraving of 1621.

what he was offered to drink, for he merely raised it to his lips, and then gave it to the others. All this was done with wonderful ceremony and with very few words, and such words as he did say, so far as I could understand them, were very formal and sensible, and those two men watched his face and they spoke for him and with him, and with great respect. After having eaten, a page brought a belt, which is like those of Castile in shape but of different workmanship, and this he took and gave to me, and two pieces of worked gold, which were very thin, so that I believe that here they obtain very little of it, although I hold that they are very near where it is found and where there is much. I saw that a drapery which I had above my bed pleased him; I gave it to him, and some very good amber beads which I was wearing round my neck, and some red shoes and a flask of orange flower water, at which he was so pleased that it was wonderful. And he and his governor and counsellors were very grieved because they did not understand me or I them. All the same I realised that he told me that, if I required anything from there, the whole island was at my disposal. I sent for some beads of mine, among which I had as a token a gold *excelente*,[83] on which Your Highnesses are depicted, and I showed this to him, and I told him again, as I had yesterday, that Your Highnesses rule and command all the best part of the world, and that there are no princes so great, and I showed him the royal standards and the others with the cross. At this he was much impressed, and he explained to his counsellors that Your Highnesses must be great sovereigns, since you had sent me from so far and from heaven without fear to this place. And many other things passed, and I did not understand anything except that I could see well that they regarded everything as wonderful." Afterwards, as it was already late, and he wished to go, the admiral sent him in the boat very honourably, and had many lombards fired, and when he had landed he entered his litter and went away with his men, who were more than two hundred, and his son was borne behind him on the shoulders of an Indian, a very honourable man. To all the sailors and people of the ships, wherever he found them, he commanded that they should be given to eat and that much honour should be paid to them. A sailor said that he had met him on the way and had seen all the things which the admiral had given to him, and all of them carried a man, who seemed to be one of the most important personages, before the king. His son followed at a good distance behind the king, with as great an escort of people as he, and so did another, a brother of the same king, except that the brother went on foot, and two principal men held him by the arm. He came to the ship after the king, and to him the admiral gave certain things of the articles of barter, and there the admiral learned that in their language they called the king "cacique." On this day, as he says, they bartered little gold, but the admiral learned from an old man that there were many islands near, at a distance of a hundred leagues or more, as far as he could understand, in which very much gold was produced, so much that the old man told him that one island was all gold and that in the others there was so great a quantity that they gather it and sift it with sieves, and they smelt it and make bars and a thousand worked articles; he explained the making by signs. This old man indicated to the admiral the direction and location of the gold; the admiral resolved to go there, and he says that, if it had not been that this old man was so important a subject of that king, he would have detained him and taken him with him. Or, if he had known the language, he says, he would have asked him to come, and he believes, as he was friendly with him and with the Christians, that he would have gone willingly. But, as he already held those people for the Sovereigns of Castile, and as there was no wisdom in offending them, he decided to let him go. He set a very mighty cross in the centre of the square of that village, in which work the Indians greatly assisted, and, as he says, they offered prayer and adored it, and from the signs which they give, the admiral hopes in Our Lord that all those islands will become Christian.

WEDNESDAY, DECEMBER 19th / This night he set sail, to go out of that gulf which the island of Tortuga there makes with Española, and when day came, the wind changed to the east, so that all this day he could not come out from between those two islands, and at night he was not able to make a harbour which appeared there. He saw near there four points of land and a large bay and river, and beyond he saw a very great bend, and there was a village and at the side a valley between many very lofty mountains: they were full of trees which he thought to be pines. Upon *Dos Hermanos*,[84] there was a very high and broad mountain, which ran from north-east to south-west; and on the east-south-east of *Cape Torres*,[85] there is a small island, which he called *Santo Tomas*,[86] because it is his vigil to-morrow. The whole circuit of that island had capes and marvellous harbours, as he judged viewing it from the sea. To the westward, before the island, there is a cape which runs far out to sea, part of it being high land and part low, for which reason he named it *Cape Alto y Bajo*.[87] To the east, east by south, from Cape Torres it is sixty miles to a mountain, higher than the other, which juts into the sea and from a distance seems to be an island apart, owing to a ravine which there is on the land side. He named it *Monte Caribata*,[88] because that province was called Caribata. It is very lovely and full of trees, a vivid green, and without snow or mists round it; and it was there at that time like March in Castile so far as the breezes and temperature were concerned, and like May for the trees and plants. He says that the nights were fourteen hours.

THURSDAY, DECEMBER 20th / To-day, at sunset, he entered a harbour which was between the island of Santo Tomas and Cape Caribata, and anchored.[89] This port is most beautiful and one in which all the ships of Christendom could lie. From the sea its entrance appears to be impossible to those who have not entered it, owing to some reefs of rocks which extend from the mountain almost as far as the island and which are not in a continuous line but are some here and some there, some being out to sea and others near the land. Consequently one has to be on watch to enter by some gaps which there are, very wide and good, so that it is possible to enter without fear; and all is very deep, seven fathoms, and when the reefs are passed, within it is twelve fathoms. The ship can be fastened with any cable against whatever winds may blow. At the entrance of this harbour he says that there was a channel, which lay to the west of a sandy island and on which there are many trees, and up to the edge of it there are seven fathoms. But there are many shoals near, and it is necessary to keep the eye open until the harbour has been entered; afterwards,

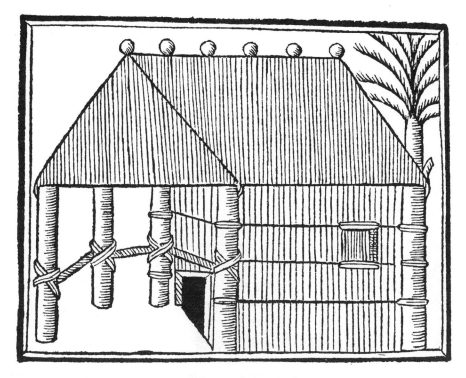

An Indian habitation; in Oviedo's *La historia general de las Indias*, 1547.

there is no fear of any tempest in the world. From that harbour, a very large valley appeared, all cultivated; it ran down to the harbour from the south-east and was all fenced in by very lofty mountains, which seemed to touch the sky, and which were very beautiful, full of green trees, and without doubt there are there loftier mountains than the island of Tenerife in the Canaries, which is held to be one of the loftiest that can be found. At a league from this part of the island of Santo Tomas there is another islet, and within that another, and in all there are wonderful harbours, but it is essential to be on the watch for shoals. He saw also some villages and the smoke which they made.

FRIDAY, DECEMBER 21st / To-day he went with the ships' boats to see that harbour. He saw it to be such that he affirms that none of those which he had ever seen equalled it. And he excuses himself, saying that as he has praised those already visited so much, he does not know how to praise this, and that he fears that he may be thought to extol excessively and out of proportion. He meets this charge, saying that he has with him old sailors, and they say and will say the same, as will all who go to sea, that is, they will assent to all the praise which he has given to the harbours already seen, and agree that it is also quite true that this is much better than all. He goes on to the following effect: "I have spent twenty-three years at sea, without coming off it for any length of time worth mentioning, and I have seen all the east and west," as he says, by going on the northern voyage, which is England, ⁹⁰ "and I have gone to Guinea, but in all these parts I have not found the perfection of these harbours . . . having found the . . . better than the other, so that I considered with great care what I have written, and again I assert that I have written well, and that now this harbour surpasses all, and in it all the ships of the world could lie and be secure, with the oldest cable on board a ship it would be held fast." From the entrance to the end of the harbour it is five leagues. He saw some very cultivated lands, although all are such, and he ordered two men to land from the boats and go to a height in order to see if there was a village, since from the sea none was visible, although on that night, about ten o'clock, certain Indians came to the ship in a canoe to see and marvel at the admiral and the Christians, and he gave them of the articles of barter, at which they were much pleased. The two Christians returned and said that from there they had seen a large village, at a short distance from the sea. The admiral ordered them to row towards the place where the village was until they came near the land. He saw some Indians who came to the seashore, and as they appeared to do so with fear, he ordered the boats to be stopped, and the Indians, whom he carried with him in the ship, to tell them that he would do them no ill. They then came nearer the sea and the admiral went nearer to the land, and when they had entirely lost their fear, so many came, men and women and children a like, that they covered the earth, giving great thanks. Some of them ran here and some there to bring us the bread which they make of *niames*, which they call *ajes*, and which is very white and good, and they brought us water in gourds and clay pitchers, made like those of

Castile, and they brought to us all that they had in the world and which they knew that the admiral desired. They did all this with such generosity of heart and such joy that it was wonderful. "And it is not to be said that because what they gave was of little value, they therefore gave it liberally," says the admiral, "for they did the same and as freely when they gave pieces of gold as when they gave a gourd of water, and it is easy to know," says the admiral, "when something is given with a great readiness to give." These are his words. "These people have no spears or darts or any other arms, nor have the others in all this island, and I hold that this island is very large. They are as naked as when their mothers gave them birth, men and women alike; for in the other lands of Juana and of the other islands women wear some cotton articles in front with which they cover their privy parts, rather like a pair of men's drawers, especially after they pass the age of twelve years, but here neither young nor old do so. And in other places all the men endeavoured to conceal their women from the Christians owing to jealousy, but here they do not. There are some very well-formed women, and they were the first to come to give thanks to Heaven and to bring whatever they had, especially things to eat, bread of *ajes*, chufa,[91] and five or six kinds of fruit," which the admiral ordered to be preserved that he might bring them to the Sovereigns. He says that the women in other places did the same before they were concealed, and the admiral everywhere ordered all his men to be careful not to offend any one in any way, and to take nothing from them against their will, and so they paid them for everything which they received from them. Finally the admiral says that it is impossible to believe that any one has seen a people with such kind hearts and so ready to give and so timorous, that they deprive themselves of everything in order to give the Christians all that they possess, and when the Christians arrive, they run at once to bring them everything. Afterwards the admiral sent six Christians to the village in order to see what it was. To these men, they did every honour that they could and knew, and gave them whatever they had, so that no doubt remained but that they believed that the admiral and all his people had come from heaven. The same was the belief of the Indians whom the admiral carried with him from the other islands, despite the fact that they had been already told

what they ought to think. After the six Christians had gone, some canoes came bringing people to ask the admiral, on behalf of a chief man,
to go to his village when he left this place. "Canoe" is a vessel in which
they navigate, and some of them are large and some small. And having
found that the village of that chief was on his way, on a point of land,
and that he was awaiting the admiral with many people, he went there;
and before he set out, there came to the shore so many people that it
was alarming, men, women and children shouting that he should not
go away but remain with them. The messengers of the other chief, who
had come to invite him, remained waiting with their canoes, so that he
should not go without coming to see the chief. And he did so; and
when the admiral came to the place where that lord was awaiting him
and had a great many things to eat, he commanded all his people to
sit down. He ordered them to carry the food they had to the boats,
where the admiral was, close to the seashore. And as he saw that the
admiral had accepted what they had brought, all or most of the Indians
started to run to the village which must have been near, to bring him
more food and parrots and other things which they had, with such
generosity of heart it was a wonder. The admiral gave them glass beads
and brass rings and hawks' bells, not because they asked for anything,
but because it seemed to him to be right, and above all, says the admiral,
because he holds them to be already Christians and to belong to the
Sovereigns of Castile more than do the peoples of Castile. And he says
that nothing was lacking save to know the language and to give them
orders, because every order that was given to them they would obey
without any opposition. The admiral went back to the ships, and the
Indians, men and women and children alike, shouted that the Christians should not go away and that they should remain with them.
When they had gone, there came after them to the ship canoes full of
them, to whom he caused much honour to be done and food to be
given, and other things which they took with them. There had also
come before another lord from the west, and many people even came
swimming, and the ship was more than a full half-league from land.
"The lord, whom I mentioned, had gone back; I sent certain persons to
see him and ask him of these islands." He received them very well and
took them with him to his village, in order to give them some large

A reptile found in the New World; in Oviedo's *La hystoria general de las Indias*, 1547.

pieces of gold: they reached a large river which the Indians crossed by swimming; the Christians could not do so, and accordingly turned back. In all this neighbourhood there are very high mountains, which seem to reach to the sky, so that the mountain of the island of Tenerife appears to be nothing in comparison with them, in height and in beauty, and all are green, full of woods, so that it is a thing of wonder. Between them there are very fair plains, and at the end of this harbour, to the south, there is a plain, so extensive that eyes cannot see its end; there is no mountain to interrupt it and it seems that it must be fifteen or twenty leagues. Through it runs a river, and it is all populated and cultivated, and is as green now as if it were in Castile in May or June, although the nights are fourteen hours long and the land is so far north. This harbour is very good whatever winds may blow, protected and deep, and all inhabited by a people very good and gentle, and without arms, good or ill. In it any ship may lie without fear that other ships might come by night to attack her, because, although the mouth may be more than two leagues wide, it is to a great extent closed by two reefs of rocks, which scarcely appear above water. In this reef, however, there is a very narrow passage, which looks as if made by hand, leaving an opening wide enough for ships to enter. At the mouth, there is a depth of seven fathoms, so far as the foot of a flat islet, which has a beach and trees at its foot. On the west side, there is the entrance; a ship can without fear come near enough to touch the shore near the rock. On the north-western side, there are three islands, and there is a great river a league from the end of this harbour. It is the best in the world; he named it *Puerto de la Mar de Santo Tomas*, because to-day is his day; he called it "mar" on account of its great extent.

SATURDAY, DECEMBER 22nd / At daybreak, he set sail to proceed on his way, in search of the islands which the Indians told him had much gold, and some of which they declared to have more gold than earth. The weather was not favourable, and he was obliged to anchor again, and he sent the boat to fish with the net. The lord of that land, who had his village near there, sent him a large canoe, full of people, and in it one of his principal servants, to ask the admiral to go with the ships to his land, telling him that he would give him all that he possessed. He sent with that servant a girdle which had hanging from it, in place of a purse, a mask of which the two ears, which were large, the tongue and the nose were of beaten gold. And as these people are of a very generous disposition, so that they give whatever is asked of them with the greatest goodwill in the world, and so that it appears that any one who asks something from them does them a great favour, as the admiral puts it, they came up to the boat and gave the girdle to a ship's boy, and then came in their canoe alongside the ship to perform their embassy. Some part of the day passed before he understood them, nor did the Indians, whom he carried with him, understand them well, since they had somewhat different words for the names of things. Finally, by means of signs, he succeeded in understanding their invitation. He resolved to leave for that place on Sunday, although he was not accustomed to set out on a Sunday, solely as a result of his piety and not on account of any superstition. But, he says, in the hope that those peoples will turn Christian, on account of the goodwill which

Nude Indians with bow and arrow; in *Epistola Albericij, De nouo mundo*, 1505.

they show, and become subject to the Sovereigns of Castile, as he holds them already to be, and that they may serve him with zeal, he wishes and endeavours to do everything to please them. Before he departed to-day he sent six men to a very large village, three leagues from there, towards the west, because on the previous day the lord of that place came to the admiral and told him that he had some pieces of gold. When the Christians arrived there, the lord of the place took the hand of the admiral's secretary, who was with them. The admiral had sent him in order that he might prevent the others from doing anything unjust to the Indians. For as the Indians were so liberal and the Spaniards so greedy and unrestrained, it was not enough for them that for a lace end and even for a bit of glass and of eathenware and for other things of no value, the Indians would give them whatever they desired, but without giving anything to them, they wished to have and to take everything. This the admiral always forbade, although the things they gave to the Christians, except the gold, were also many things of small value. But the admiral, considering the generous hearts of the Indians, who for six glass beads would give and gave a piece of gold, on this account ordered that nothing should be accepted from them without something being given in exchange. So the lord of the place took the hand of the secretary and brought him to his house with all the people, who were very numerous and who accompanied him, and caused them to be given to eat, and all the Indians brought to them many things of cotton, worked and wound into small balls. Later in the afternoom, the lord of the place gave them three very fat geese and some small pieces of gold. A great number of people came with them and carried all the things which they had exchanged there, and they contended among themselves for the honour of carrying them on their backs, and in fact they did so carry the Christians across some rivers and through some marshy places. The admiral ordered some things to be given to the lord of the place, and he and all his people were very content, firmly believing that they had come from heaven, and they regarded themselves as fortunate in having seen the Christians. On this day more than a hundred and twenty canoes came to the ships, all being full of people, and they all brought something, especially their bread and fish, and water in small earthenware jars, and seeds of many kinds, which are good spices. They threw a grain into a mug of water and drank it, and the Indians, whom the admiral carried with him, said that it was a most healthy thing.

SUNDAY, DECEMBER 23rd / For lack of wind the admiral could not leave with the ships for the land of that lord who had sent to ask him and invite him to come, but with the three messengers who waited there, he sent the boats with people and the secretary. While these were on their way, he sent two of the Indians, whom he had with him, to the

villages which were near there close to the station of the ships, and
they returned with a lord to the ship with news that in the island of
Española there was a great quantity of gold, and that they came from
other places to buy it, and they told him that there he might have as
much as he wished. Others came who confirmed the statement that in
it there was much gold, and they showed him the method which they
used to collect it. All this the admiral understood with difficulty, but
yet he regarded it as clear that in those parts there was a very great
quantity of gold and that, if the place where it was procured were
found, he would get it very cheaply and, as he imagined, for nothing.
And he repeats that he believes there must be much, because during
the three days he was in that harbour he had secured good pieces
of gold, and it could not be believed that they brought it there from
another land. "Our Lord, Who holds all things in His hand, be pleased
to aid me and to give whatever may be for His service." These are
the words of the admiral. He says that at that hour he believes that
more than a thousand persons had come to the ship, and that all
brought some of the things they possess, and that, before they have
come within half a crossbow shot of the ship, they stand up in their
canoes, and take what they bring in their hands, crying, "Take! Take!"
He also believes that more than five hundred came to the ship swimming, because they had no canoes; and the ship was anchored about
a league from the shore. He estimated that five lords and sons of
lords with their whole household, women and children, had come there
to see the Christians. The admiral ordered something to be given to all,
for he says that this was all well spent, and he says: "Our Lord in His
Goodness guide me that I may find this gold, I mean their mine, for
I have many here who say that they know it." These are his words.
In the night the boats arrived, and they said that their journey had
been a long one, and that at the mountain of Caribata they found many
canoes with many people, who came to see the admiral and the Christians from the place to which the latter were going, and he was sure
that if he could be in that harbour on the feast of the Nativity, all the
people of that island, which he now estimated as being larger than
England, would come to see them. All these returned with the Christians to the village, which, he says, they declared to be larger and

better laid out in streets than any of those previously found up to then. He says that this village lies about three leagues to the south-east of Punta Santa, and as the canoes can be rowed fast, they went ahead to give the news to the "cacique," as they call him there. Up to that time the admiral had not been able to understand whether by this they meant "king" or "governor." They use also another name for a "grandee," whom they call "nitayno"; he did not know if by this they mean "hidalgo" or "governor" or "judge." The cacique finally came to them, and they gathered in the square, which was very clean; the whole village, which contained more than two thousand men, was there. This king did much honour to the people from the ships, and the common people, each one of them, gave them something to eat and drink. Afterwards, the king gave to each one some cotton cloths, which the women wear, and parrots for the admiral, and some pieces of gold. The common people also presented some of the same cloths and other things from their houses to the sailors, in return for a trifle which they gave them and which, judging from the way they received it, they seemed to regard as relics. When it was evening and they wished to depart, the king asked them to wait until the next day, as did all the people. When it was clear that they were resolved to go, the Indians went a long distance with them, carrying the things which the cacique and the others had given them on their backs to the boats, which remained at the mouth of the river.

MONDAY, DECEMBER 24th / Before sunrise, he weighed anchor with a land breeze. Among the many Indians who had come yesterday to the ship and who had indicated to them that there was gold in that island and had named the places where it was collected, he saw one who seemed to be better disposed and more attached to him, or who spoke to him with more pleasure. He flattered this man and asked him to go with him to show him the mines of gold. This Indian brought another, a friend or relation, with him, and among the other places which they named where gold was found, they spoke of Cipangu, which they call "Cibao," and they declared that there was a great quantity of gold there, and that the cacique carries banners of beaten gold, but that it is very far to the east. The admiral here says these words to the

The Indian method of making wine; in Benzoni's *Historia del Mondo Nuovo*, 1563.

Sovereigns: "Your Highnesses may believe that in all the world there cannot be a people better or more gentle. Your Highnesses should feel great joy, because they will presently become Christians and will be educated in the good customs of your realms, for there cannot be a better people or country, and the number of the people and the extent of the country are so great that I no longer know how to describe them. For I have spoken in the superlative of the people and land of Juana, which they call Cuba, but there is as great a difference between that and this as there is between night and day. Nor do I believe that any one who had seen this would have done or said less than I have said and say. For it is true that the things here are a wonder, and the great peoples of this island of Española, for so I call it, and they call it 'Bohio,' all display the most extraordinarily gentle behaviour and have soft voices, unlike the others, who seem to threaten when they talk; and they are, men and women, of good height and not black. It is true that they all paint themselves, some black, and others with some other colour, and the majority red. (I have learned that they do this on account of the sun, so that it may not harm them so much.) The houses and villages are so lovely, and in all there is government, with a judge or lord of them, and all obey him so that it is a wonder. And all these lords are men of few words and excellent manners, and their method of giving orders is generally to make signs with the hand, and it is understood, so that it is a marvel." All these are the words of the admiral. Any one who has to enter the sea of Santo Tomas must steer a full league over the mouth of the entrance, by a small flat island which lies in the middle of it, which he called *la Amiga*, [92] keeping the bow towards it. After coming within a stone's throw of it, he must pass to the west of it and leave it to the east, and must keep near it and not go in the other direction, as a very large reef stretches from the west and even out to sea; beyond it, there are three shoals, and this reef comes to within a lombard shot of La Amiga. He must pass between the reef and the island, and he will find at the shallowest point seven fathoms, and gravel beneath, and within he will find a harbour for all the ships in the world, where they may lie without cables. Another reef and shoals extend from the east to the island of La Amiga, and are very large and stretch far out to sea and come within two leagues of the cape, but between them it appeared that there was a passage, at two lombard shots from La Amiga; and at the foot of Mount Caribata, towards the west, there is a very good harbour and very large. [93]

TUESDAY, DECEMBER 25th: CHRISTMAS DAY / He navigated with little wind yesterday from the sea of Santo Tomas towards Punta Santa, [94] from which he was distant one league when the first quarter had passed, that is, at eleven o'clock at night, and he decided to lie down to sleep, because for two days and a night he had not slept. As it was calm, the sailor, who was steering the ship, decided to go to sleep, and he left the steering to a young ship's boy, a thing which the admiral had always strictly forbidden during the whole voyage, whether there was

The *Santa Maria*; model after the plans of E. D'Albertis.

a wind or whether it was calm, that is to say, they were not to leave
the steering to ships' boys. The admiral felt secure from banks and
rocks, because on Sunday, when he sent the boats to that king, they
had passed a full three leagues and a half to the east of Punta Santa,
and the sailors had seen all the coast and the shoals from Punta Santa
to the east-south-east for a full three leagues, and they had found where
it was possible to pass, which he had not done during the whole voyage.
Our Lord willed that at midnight, as they had seen the admiral lie
down and rest, and as they saw that it was a dead calm and the sea
was as in a bowl, all should lie down to sleep, and the rudder was left
in the hand of that boy, and the currents carried the ship upon one
of those banks; [95] the sea breaking on them made so much noise that it
could be heard and seen, although it was night, at a full league's
distance. The ship went upon it so gently that it was hardly noticed.
The boy, who felt the rudder ground, and heard the sound of the sea,

shouted, and at his cries, the admiral came out and was so quick that
no one had yet realized that they were aground. Immediately the
master of the ship, whose watch it was, came out, and the admiral told
him and the others to launch the boat which they carried at the stern,
to take an anchor and throw it out astern, and he with many others
jumped into the boat, and the admiral thought that they were doing
what he had ordered them to do. They only thought of escaping
to the caravel, which was lying half a league to windward. The
caravel would not take them aboard, therein acting rightly, and on
this account they returned to the ship, but the boat of the caravel
reached her first. When the admiral saw that they were running away
and that it was his crew, and that the water was growing shallower
and the ship was now lying broadside on to the sea, as he saw
no other remedy, he ordered the mast to be cut and the ship to be
lightened as far as possible to see whether they could draw her
off. And as the water became shallower still, he was unable to
save her, and she lay on her side, broadside on to the sea, although
there was little or no sea running, and then the seams opened, but the
ship remained whole. The admiral went to the caravel, in order to
place the crew of the ship in safety on the caravel, and as a light breeze
was now blowing from land, and there also still remained much of
the night and they did not know how far the banks extended, he hung
off until it was day and then went to the ship from within the line of
the bank. He had first sent the boat ashore with Diego de Arana of
Cordoba, alguacil [96] of the fleet, and Pero Gutierrez, butler of the royal
household, to inform the king who on Saturday night had sent him
an invitation and asked him to come to his harbour with the ships,
and who had his town about a league and a half away from the bank. [97]
When he heard the news, they say that he wept and sent all his people
from the town, with many large canoes to unload the ship. This was
done and everything was taken from the decks in a very short space
of time. So great was the haste and diligence which that king showed!
And he in person, with his brothers and relatives, was active both
on the ship and in guarding what was brought to land, so that everything might be very safely kept. From time to time, he sent one of

Natives of the New World; a woodcut of 1521-22.

his relatives in tears to the admiral, to console him, telling him that he must not be troubled or annoyed, that he would give him whatever he possessed. The admiral assures the Sovereigns that nowhere in Castile could he have been able to place everything in greater security, without the loss of a shoe string. He commanded everything to be placed near the houses, while some houses which he wished to give were emptied, that there everything might be placed and guarded. He ordered armed men to be set round everything to keep watch all night. "He and all the people with him wept. They are," says the admiral, "a people so full of love and without greed, and suitable for every purpose, that I assure Your Highnesses that I believe there is no better race or better land in the world. They love their neighbours as themselves, and they have the softest and gentlest voices in the world, and they are always smiling. They go naked, men and women, as their mothers bore them. But Your Highnesses may believe that in their intercourse with one another they have very good customs, and the king maintains a very marvellous state, of a style so orderly that it is a pleasure to see it, and they have good memories and they wish to see everything and ask what it is and for what it is used." All this says the admiral.

WEDNESDAY, DECEMBER 26th / To-day at sunrise the king of that land, who was in that village, came to the caravel *Niña*, where the admiral was, and, almost in tears, told him that he must not be grieved, for he would give him whatever he had, and that he had given to the Christians who were on shore two very large houses, and that he would give them more if it were necessary, and as many canoes as they needed to load and unload the ship and bring to land as many men as he might wish, as had been done yesterday without a crumb of bread being taken or anything else at all. "They are so loyal," says the admiral, "and without greed for what is not theirs, and so above all the others was that virtuous king." While the admiral was talking with him, another canoe came from another direction, which brought certain pieces of gold, which they wanted to give for a hawk's bell, because they wish for nothing so much as for hawks' bells. So while the canoe had not yet reached the ship's side, they called out and showed the pieces of gold, crying "chuque chuque," meaning hawks' bells, for they almost go crazy for them. After they saw this and the canoes which came from other places were about to leave, they called the admiral and asked him to have a hawk's bell kept until next day, since they would bring him four pieces of gold as large as the hand. The admiral rejoiced to hear this, and afterwards a sailor, who came from ashore, told the admiral that it was wonderful to see the pieces of gold which the Christians who were on land were getting in exchange for nothing; for a leather thong they gave pieces of gold worth more than two castellanos, and this was nothing to what it would be at the end of a month. The king was greatly delighted to see the admiral joyful and understood that he desired much gold, and he told him by signs that he knew where there was very much in great abundance near there, and that he should be of good cheer, for he would give him as much gold as he might desire. He says that he explained this to him, and more particularly that in Cipangu, which they called "Cibao," it was in such quantity that they regard it as of no account, and that he would bring it from there, although in that island of Española, which they call "Bohio," and in that province of Caribata, there is also very much. The king ate in the caravel with the admiral, and afterwards landed with him, and on land did the admiral much honour, and gave him a repast of two or three kinds of *ajes* and with them shrimps and game, and other foods which they had, and some of their bread which they call "cacabi." [98] Thence he took him to see some groves of trees near the houses, and about a thousand people, all naked, went there with him. The king now wore a shirt and gloves, which the admiral had given him, and he rejoiced more over the gloves than over anything which had been given to him. In his eating, by his decent behaviour and exquisite cleanliness, he showed clearly that he was of good birth. After having eaten, as he remained at the table for some while, they brought him some herbs with which he rubbed his hands a great deal. The admiral believed that he did so in order to make them soft, and they gave him water for his hands. After they had finished eating, he brought the admiral to the beach, and the admiral sent for a Turkish bow and a handful of arrows, and caused a man of his company to shoot them; he was skilful, and the chief was very much impressed, as he did not know what weapons are, since they neither have nor use them. The admiral says, however, that the beginning of it all was talk about the people of Caniba, whom they call "Caribs," who come to capture them and carry bows and arrows, without iron; for in all those lands there is no knowledge of it or of steel, or of any other metal, except gold and copper, although the admiral had only seen a little copper. The admiral told him by signs that the Sovereigns of Castile would order the destruction of the Caribs and would have them all brought with their hands bound.

The admiral ordered a lombard and a musket to be fired, and seeing
the effect which their force had and what they pierced, the chief was
left wondering; and when his people heard the firing, they all fell
on the ground. They brought to the admiral a large mask, which had
great pieces of gold in the ears and eyes and in other places, and this
was given to him with other gold ornaments, which the king himself
placed on the admiral's head and round his neck; and to the other
Christians who were with him he also gave many things. The admiral
was greatly pleased and consoled with these things which he saw, and
the grief and pain which he had suffered and continued to suffer for
the loss of the ship was assuaged, and he recognised that Our Lord
had caused the ship to run aground there in order that a settlement
might there be formed. "And," he says, "in addition to this, so many
things came to hand, that in truth it was no disaster, but rather
great good fortune; for it is certain," he says, "that had I not run
aground there, I should have kept out to sea without anchoring at
this place, because it is situated within a large bay and in that bay
there are two or more sandbanks; and on this voyage I should not
have left people here, and, had I desired to leave them, I could not
have given them so many supplies, stores and provisions, nor the
material needed for making a fort. And it is very true that many of the
people who are with me have asked and petitioned that I give them
permission to remain. Now I have ordered a tower and fortress
to be built, all very well done, and a large moat, " not that I believe it
to be necessary for these people, for I take it for granted that with
these men whom I have with me I could subdue all this island, which
I believe to be larger than Portugal and with more than twice the
population. But they are all naked and without arms and very cowardly
beyond hope of change. It is right, however, that this tower should
be built, and it must be as it must be, being so distant from Your Highnesses, and in order that they may realise the skill of the people of
Your Highnesses and what they can do, so that they may serve them
with love and fear. So they have boards with which to construct the
whole fortress, and provisions of bread and wine for more than a
year, and seeds to sow, and the ship's boat and a caulker and a carpenter
and a gunner and a cooper, and many men among them who are

The fort at Navidad; in the illustrated edition of the Columbus letter, 1493.

very zealous in the service of Your Highnesses, and who will give me the pleasure of finding the mine where the gold is collected. Thus, then, all has happened greatly to the purpose that a beginning may be made, and above all, when the ship ran aground, it was so gently that the shock was hardly felt, and there was no sea or wind." All this the admiral says, and he adds more, in order to show that it was great good fortune and the predestined will of God that the ship should run aground there, so that he would leave people there; and if it had not been for the disloyalty of the master, and of the crew, who were all, or most of them from his district, in being unwilling to throw out the anchor from the stern in order to drag off the ship, as the admiral commanded them, the ship would have been saved, and so he would not have been able to learn about the land, he says, as he learned in those days that he was there, and as he will learn later, through those whom he resolved to leave there. For it was always with the intention of discovering that he voyaged and not delaying more than a day in any place, save for lack of wind, but he says that the ship was very slow and not suited to the work of discovery. He says that it was the men of Palos who caused such a ship to be taken, for they did not fulfil what they had promised to the King and Queen in supplying ships suitable for that voyage. The admiral ends by saying that of all that was in the ship not a leather thong nor a plank nor a nail was lost, because she remained as sound as when she set out, except that she was cut and split to some extent in order to get out the water butts and all the cargo, and they brought everything to land and had it well guarded, as has been said. And he says that he trusts in God that on his return, which he intended to make from Castile, he would find a barrel of gold, which those whom he had left there should have obtained by barter, and they would have found the gold mine and the spices, and in such quantity, that the Sovereigns, within three years, would undertake and prepare to go to the conquest of the Holy Places, "For so," he says, "I protested to Your Highnesses that all the gain of this my enterprise should be expended on the conquest of Jerusalem, and Your Highnesses smiled and said that it pleased them, and that without this they had that inclination." These are the words of the admiral.

THURSDAY, DECEMBER 27th / At sunrise, the king of that land came to the caravel and told the admiral that he had sent for gold and that he desired to clothe him in gold before he departed; but rather, he begged him not to depart. And with the admiral there were the king and his brother and another relative, very high in favour, and these two men told him that they wished to go to Castile with him. At this juncture, certain Indians came with the news that the caravel *Pinta* was in a river at the end of that island. The cacique at once dispatched a canoe there, and in it the admiral sent a sailor; for he so greatly loved the admiral that it was a marvel. The admiral already intended to prepare for his return to Castile with as much speed as he could.

FRIDAY, DECEMBER 28th / In order to direct and hasten the completion of the building of the fortress and to give directions to the people who were to remain in it, the admiral landed, and it appeared to him that the king had seen him while he was still in the boat, for he at once went into his house, dissembling, and sent his brother to greet the admiral and bring him to one of the houses which he had given to the admiral's people, the largest and best in that town. In it they had prepared a dais of the inner bark of palm trees, where they caused him to seat himself. Afterwards, the brother sent one of his pages to tell the king that the admiral was there, as if the king was unaware that he had come, although the admiral believed that he made pretence to do him much greater honour. When the page delivered his message, as he says, the cacique hurried to come to the admiral, and placed round his neck a great plate of gold which he carried in his hand. He remained there with him until evening, considering what was to be done.

SATURDAY, DECEMBER 29th / At sunrise, there came to the caravel a nephew of the king, very young and of good understanding and courage, as the admiral says, and as he always endeavoured to learn where they gathered the gold, he asked every one, for by means of signs he now understood something. And so this youth told him that four days' journey to the east there was an island which was called "Guarioné," and others which were called "Maricorix," and "Mayonic," and "Fuma," and "Cibao," and "Coroay," in which there was infinite gold. The admiral wrote these names down, and when the brother of the king heard what the youth had said, he rebuked him, as the admiral gathered. On other occasions also the admiral had understood that the king endeavoured to prevent him from learning where the gold originated and was collected, in order that he might not go elsewhere to barter for it or buy it. "But there is so much and in so many places, and in this island of Española itself," says the admiral, "that it is a wonder." When it was already night, the king sent him a great mask of gold, and sent to him also to ask for a hand-basin and a jar. The admiral believed that he asked this so as to have others made, and so he sent him what he asked for.

SUNDAY, DECEMBER 30th / The admiral went ashore to eat, and he arrived just as there had come five kings, subject to him who was called Guacanagarí, all with their crowns, an indication of very high estate, so that the admiral tells the Sovereigns that their Highnesses would have been pleased to see their bearing. As he reached land, the king came to receive the admiral and led him by the arm to the same house as yesterday, where there was a dais and chairs, on which he placed the admiral, and immediately took the crown from his own head, and placed it on that of the admiral. And the admiral took from his neck a collar of good bloodstones and very beautiful beads, of very fine colour, which appeared very good in every way, and placed it round his neck, and he took off a cloak of rich scarlet cloth which he was wearing that day, and dressed him in it. And he sent for some coloured buskins which he made him put on, and placed on his finger a large silver ring, because they had told him that he had seen a sailor with a silver ring and had tried hard to obtain it. He was very pleased and very content, and two of those kings, who were with him, came to where the admiral was beside him, and brought to the admiral two large plates of gold, each bringing one. And just then, there came an Indian, saying that two days before he had left the caravel *Pinta* to the east in a harbour. The admiral went back to the caravel, and Vincente Yañez, her captain, declared that he had seen rhubarb and that it was in the island Amiga, which is at the entrance of the sea of Santo Tomas, six leagues from there, and that he had recognised

The cacao tree; in Benzoni's *Historia del Mondo Nuovo*, 1563.

the branches and root. They say that rhubarb throws out small branches from the ground, and that it has some fruit which looks like green mulberries, almost dry, and that the stalk in the part near the root is as yellow and as fine as the best colour there can be to paint; and underground it has a root like a large pear.

MONDAY, DECEMBER 31st / On this day, he concerned himself with ordering water and wood to be taken in for his departure for Spain, in order to give speedy news to the Sovereigns, that they might send ships to discover what remained to be discovered, since already the matter appeared, says the admiral, to be so great and of such moment as to be a marvel. And he says that he did not wish to depart until he had seen all that land which there was towards the east and gone along all the coast, in order to learn also the length of the journey from Castile there, he says, for the purpose of bringing stock and other things. But, as he was left with only one ship, it did not seem to him reasonable to expose himself to the dangers which he might encounter in the course of discovery; and he complained that all this evil and inconvenience was the result of the caravel *Pinta* having parted from him.

TUESDAY, JANUARY 1st / At midnight he dispatched the boat to the islet of Amiga to fetch the rhubarb. It returned at vespers with a basket of it. They did not bring more, because they had no spade to dig; he brought this as a specimen to the Sovereigns. The king of that land said that he had sent many canoes for gold. There returned the canoe, which went to get news of the *Pinta*, and the sailor, and they had not found her. The sailor said that twenty leagues from there they had seen a king who wore two large plates of gold on his head, and immediately the Indians in the canoe had spoken to him, he took them off. He also saw much gold on other persons. The admiral believed that king Guacanagarí must have forbidden all to sell gold to the Christians, in order that all might pass through his hands. But he had learned the places, as he said the day before yesterday, where it was in such quantity that they held it to be of no account. Moreover the spice, which they eat, says the admiral, is in large amount and more valuable than pepper or allspice. He left orders to those whom he wished to leave there that they should procure as much as they could.

WEDNESDAY, JANUARY 2nd / He landed in the morning in order to take leave of king Guacanagarí and to set out in the name of the Lord, and he gave him one of his shirts. And he showed him the power which the lombards had and the effect which they produced, and for this purpose he ordered one to be loaded and fired at the side of the ship which was aground. This was as a result of a conversation concerning the Caribs, with whom they were at war; and he saw how far the lombard carried, and how it pierced the side of the ship, and how the charge went far out to sea. He also had the people of the ships arm themselves and engage in a sham fight, telling the cacique that he was not to fear the Caribs even if they should come. All this

A cactus plant; in Ramusio's *Navigationi et Viaggi*, 1606.

the admiral says that he did, that the king might regard the Christians whom he left as friends and might be frightened and have fear of them. The admiral took him with him to eat at the house where he was lodged, and the others who went with him. The admiral greatly recommended to him Diego de Arana and Pero Gutierrez and Rodrigo Escovedo, whom he was leaving as his joint lieutenants over the people who remained there, in order that all might be well regulated and organised for the service of God and of their Highnesses. The cacique showed great affection for the admiral and great grief at his departure, especially when he saw him go to embark. A favourite of that king told the admiral that he had commanded a statue of pure gold, as large as the admiral himself, to be made, and that in ten days they would bring it. The admiral embarked with the intention of setting out at once, but the wind did not permit him to do so. He left in that island of Española, which the Indians call "Bohio," thirty-nine men in the fortress, and he says that they were very friendly with that king Guacanagarí. Over them, as his lieutenants, he left Diego de Arana, a native of Cordoba, and Pero Gutierrez, butler of the king's dais, a subordinate of the *despensaro mayor*,[100] and Rodrigo de Esco-vedo, a native of Segovia, nephew of Fray Rodrigo Perez, with all his powers which he held from the Sovereigns. He left with them all the merchandise which the Sovereigns commanded to be bought for purposes of barter, and this was much, in order that they might deal and exchange it for gold, with all that had been brought from the ship. He left them also bread, biscuit for a year, and wine, and much artillery, and the ship's boat, in order that they, being sailors as most of them were, might go, when they saw a suitable time, to discover the mine of gold, so that, when the admiral returned, much gold might be collected by his coming, and a place found where a town might be established, because this was not a harbour after his heart, especially because the gold which they brought there came, as he says, from the east, and the more they were to the east, the nearer they were to Spain. He left them also some seeds to sow, and his officials, the secretary and the alguacil, and with them a ship's carpenter and a caulker and a good gunner, who well understood machines, and a cooper, and a doctor, and a tailor, and all, as he says, seamen.

THURSDAY, JANUARY 3rd / He did not set out to-day, because at night, he says, three of the Indians whom he brought from the islands, and who had remained, came and said that the others and their women would come at sunrise. The sea also was rather rough and the boat could not go to land. He resolved to depart on the next day, the grace of God allowing. He said that if he had had with him the caravel

How the Indians sleep; in Benzoni's *Historia del Mondo Nuovo*, 1563.

Pinta, he would certainly have been able to bring back a barrel of gold, for he would have dared to go along the coasts of these islands, a thing which he did not dare to do being alone, lest some accident should occur to him and prevent him from returning to Castile and from informing the Sovereigns of all the things which he had found. And if it were certain that the caravel *Pinta*, with that Martin Alonso Pinzón, would reach Spain safely, he said that he would not abandon doing what he desired; but, since he heard nothing from him, and because, when he went, he might tell lies to the Sovereigns in order to avoid the punishment which he deserved, as he had done and was doing so much harm in going away without permission and in preventing the good which might have been achieved and learned at that time, says the admiral, he trusted that Our Lord would give him fair weather and that all would be remedied.

FRIDAY, JANUARY 4th / At sunrise, he weighed anchor with a light wind, and the boat led the way towards the north-west, in order to get outside the reef by another channel, wider than that by which he entered. This channel and others are very good for going beyond the town of La Navidad, and everywhere there the least depth which he found was from three to nine fathoms. These two extend from the north-west to the south-east, for those shoals were great and stretch from Cape Santo to Cape de Sierpe,[101] which is more than six leagues, and outside to sea the depth is a good three fathoms, and by Cape Santo, at a league's distance, there is not more than eight fathoms' depth, and within the said cape, to the east, there are many shallows and channels by which to pass through them. All that coast trends to the north-west and south-east, and is all sandy and the land very flat, as far as a full four leagues inland. Afterwards, there are very high mountains, and all is thickly populated with large villages, and they are good people, as they proved themselves to be towards the Christians. So he navigated to the east, in the direction of a very high mountain, which appears to be an island, but is not, for it has a very low-lying isthmus uniting it with the shore. It is shaped like a very lovely pavilion, and he called it *Monte Christi*;[102] it lies exactly to the east of Cape Santo, and at a distance of eighteen leagues. On that day, since the wind was very light, he could not come within six leagues of Monte Christi. He found four very low sandy islets, with a reef which stretched far to the north-west and went far to the south-east. Within it, there is a very large gulf, which extends from the said mountain to the south-east a full twenty leagues, and this must be all very shallow and have many banks. Within it on all the coast there are many rivers, not navigable, although that sailor whom the admiral sent with the canoe to learn news of the caravel *Pinta*, said that he saw a river into which ships might enter. The admiral anchored there six leagues from Monte Christi, in nineteen fathoms, having put out to sea in order to keep away from the many shoals and reefs that were there, and he remained there that night. The admiral warns that he who has to go to the town of La Navidad when sighting Monte Christi, should keep two leagues out to sea, etc. But, because that land is already known, and more in that direction, it is not set down here. He concludes that Cipangu is on that island, and that there is much gold and spice and mastic and rhubarb.

SATURDAY, JANUARY 5th / When the sun was about to rise, he set sail with a land breeze; afterwards the wind changed to the east, and he saw that to the south-south-east of Monte Christi, between it and a small island, there seemed to be a good harbour in which to anchor for the night. He steered to the east-south-east, and afterwards to the south-south-east, a good six leagues towards the mountain, and he found, when the six leagues had been accomplished, seventeen fathoms' depth and soft bottom, and so he went three leagues with the same depth. Afterwards, the depth lessened to twelve fathoms in the direction of the head of the mountain, and off the head of the mountain, at a league's distance, he found nine fathoms, and all clear, with fine sand. So he followed his course, until he entered between the mountain and the islet, where he found three and a half fathoms' depth, at low tide, and a very remarkable harbour, where he anchored. He went with the boat to the islet, where he found a fire and evidence that fishermen had been there. He saw there many coloured stones of various shades, or a quarry of such stones, naturally shaped, very lovely, he says, for church buildings or for other royal works, like those which he found in the islet of San Salvador. He also found in this islet many roots of mastic. He says that this Monte Christi is very beautiful and lofty and accessible, of a very attractive form, and all the land near it is low, very fair cultivable land, and it alone is so high that, being seen from a distance, it looks like an island without connection with any land. Beyond the mountain, to the east, he saw a cape at a distance of twenty-four miles, which he called *Cape Bezerro*,[103] and from it as far as the mountain some reefs with shallows stretch out to sea a good two leagues. It seems, however, that there were between them channels by which an entry might be made, but it is well that it should be by day and that the attempt should be made with the boat going ahead to take soundings. From this mountain, to the east, towards Cape Bezerro, for four leagues, it is all beach, and the land is very low and beautiful, and for the rest the whole country is very high, and there are great mountains, cultivated and lovely, and inland a chain runs from the north-east to the south-east, the most lovely that he had seen, so that it seemed like the sierra of Cordoba. Very far away there appeared also other mountains, very lofty, towards the south and the south-east, and very large valleys, very green and very beautiful, and many streams; all this is in such delightful quantity, that he did not believe that he had exaggerated a thousandth part. Afterwards, he saw to the east of the said mountain a land, which seemed to be another mountain, like Monte Christi in greatness and beauty, and from there, to the north-east by east, the land is not so high, and it must be a full hundred miles, or about that.

SUNDAY, JANUARY 6th / That harbour is sheltered from all winds, except the north and north-west, and he says that they prevail little in that land, and that even from these winds they can be protected behind the islet; there is from three to four fathoms' depth. At sunrise, he set sail to go farther along the coast, which trended continually eastward, only it is necessary to give wide berth to the many reefs of rock and sand which are on this coast. It is true that within them there are good harbours and good entrances through their channels. After midday, the east wind blew freshly; and he ordered a sailor to go up the mast to watch for shallows. He saw the caravel *Pinta* coming towards him from the east, and she reached the admiral, and since there was nowhere to anchor, as it was shallow water, the admiral returned to Monte Christi, going back the ten leagues which he had made, and the *Pinta* with him. Martin Alonso Pinzón came to the caravel *Niña*, in which the admiral was, to excuse himself, saying that he had parted from him against his will and giving reasons for this. But the admiral says that they were all false, and that he had gone away that night when he had left him with much haughtiness and greed; and the admiral says that he did not know the cause of the arrogance and disloyalty with which he had used him during that voyage. This the admiral wished to pass over in order not to give room for the evil works of Satan, who greatly desired to hinder the

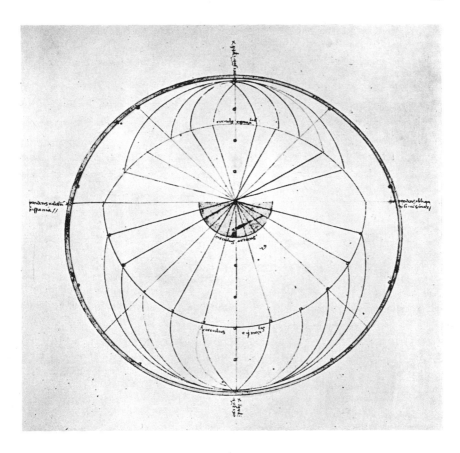

Planisphere drawn by Columbus; postille in Enea Piccolomini, *Historia rerum ubique gestarum*.

voyage, as he had done up to that time. But an Indian, one of those whom the admiral had entrusted to him, with others whom he carried in his caravel, had told Martin Alonso that in an island which was called "Baneque" there was much gold, and as he had a handy and light vessel, he wished to part company and to go by himself, leaving the admiral, but the admiral was anxious to wait and to coast along the islands of Juana and Española, since all that voyage would be to the east. After Martin Alonso had gone to the island of Baneque, he says, and found no gold, he came to the coast of Española, as a result of information received from other Indians, who told him that in that island of Española, which the Indians called "Bohio," there was a great quantity of gold and many mines, and on this account he arrived near the town of La Navidad, some fifteen leagues from it, and that was more than twenty days ago. From this it seems that the news, which the Indians gave, was true, on account of which king Guacanagarí sent the canoe and the admiral the sailor, and that he must have gone away when the canoe arrived. And the admiral says here that the caravel bartered for much gold, so that for a lace tip they gave good pieces of gold, the size of two fingers, and sometimes the size of a hand, and Martin Alonso took half and divided the other half among his men. The admiral goes on telling the Sovereigns: "Thus, Sovereign Princes, I realise that Our Lord miraculously ordained that the ship should remain there, because it is the best place in all the island for forming a settlement and nearest to the mines of gold." He says also that he learned that behind the island of Juana, towards the south, there is another great island, in which there is a greater quantity of gold than in this, to such an extent that they collected nuggets larger than beans, and in the island of Española they gathered pieces of gold from the mines as large as grains of wheat. That island, he says, was called "Yamaye."[104] The admiral also says that he learned that towards the east, there was an island where there were none save women only, and he says that he learned this from many persons, and that the island of Española or the other island of Yamaye was distant from the mainland ten days' journey in a canoe, which must be sixty or seventy leagues, and that there the people were clothed.

MONDAY, JANUARY 7th / This day he had the caravel, which was leaking, pumped and caulked, and the sailors went ashore to collect wood, and he says that they found much mastic and lignaloe.

TUESDAY, JANUARY 8th / As there was a strong east and south-easterly wind blowing, he did not set out on this day. Accordingly, he ordered that the caravel should take in supplies of water and wood and all that was necessary for the whole voyage, because, although he was anxious to coast along the whole shore of Española, which, keeping to his course, he could have done, yet those whom he had

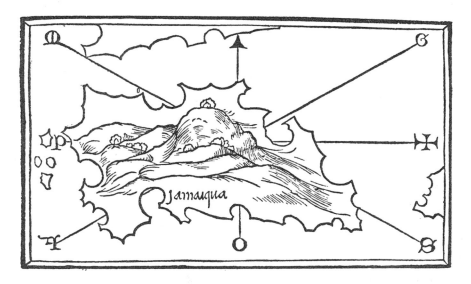

The island of Jamaica; in Bordone's *Isolario*, 1528.

placed in the caravels as captains, who were brothers, that is to say, Martin Alonso Pinzón and Vicente Yañez, and others who followed them, considering with haughtiness and greed that all was now their own, disregarding the honour which the admiral had done and given to them, had not obeyed and did not obey his commands, but on the contrary did and said many unjust things against him, and Martin Alonso had left him from the twenty-first of November until the sixth of January without cause or reason, but only out of disobedience. All this the admiral had suffered and overlooked in order to bring his voyage to a good conclusion; therefore, in order to free himself from such evil company, in which, he says, he was compelled to dissemble, although they were a disobedient people and although he had with him many men of goodwill, but it was not the time to consider punishment, he resolved to return with the greatest haste possible, and not to delay any further. He entered the boat and went to the river, which is near there, a full league towards the south-south-east of Monte Christi, where the sailors had gone to take water for the ship, and he found that the sand at the mouth of the river, which, he says, is very large and deep, was all full of gold and of such quality that it was a wonder, although it was very small. The admiral believed that in coming down that river it crumbled on the way, although he says that in a little space he found many grains as large as lentils, but the smaller size, he says, was in great abundance. And, as the sea was at high tide and the salt water mingled with the fresh, he ordered the boat to go up the river a stone's-throw. They filled the water butts from the boat, and returning to the caravel, they found caught in the hoops of the barrels small pieces of gold, and the same thing in the hoops of the cask. The admiral called the river *Rio del Oro*,[105] and within, when the entrance has been passed, it is very deep, although the entrance is shallow, and the mouth is very wide, and it is seventeen leagues from the town of La Navidad. In the interval there are other large rivers, and especially three, which he believed must have much more gold than that, because they are larger, although this is as large as the Guadalquivir at Cordoba, and from them to the mines of gold it is not twenty leagues. The admiral says further that he did not wish to take any of that sand which contained so much gold, because their Highnesses had it all under their absolute control and at the gate of their town of La Navidad, but first to come at full speed to bring them the news and to escape from the evil company which he had, and he had always said that they were a disobedient people.

WEDNESDAY, JANUARY 9th / At midnight he set sail with the wind south-east and steered to the east-north-east. He reached a headland, which he called *Punta Roja*,[106] which is exactly to the east of Monte Christi, sixty miles away, and in the shelter of it he anchored in the afternoon at approximately three hours before nightfall. He did not dare to leave there by night, because there were many reefs, until they were known, for afterwards they would be an advantage, if they had channels, as they must have, and would have great depth of water and good anchorage, secure from all winds. These lands, from Monte Christi to the point where he anchored, are high and smooth and very fair champaign, and at the sides there are very lovely mountains, which run from east to west, and are all tilled and green, so that it is a wonder to see their beauty, and there are many streams. In all this

The presentation of a book to Isabel and Ferdinand of Spain; a woodcut of 1502.

land there are many tortoises, some of which, as they had come ashore to lay their eggs, the sailors took at Monte Christi, and they were as large as a wooden shield. The day before, when the admiral went to the Rio del Oro, he said that he saw three sirens, who rose very high from the sea, but they were not as beautiful as they are depicted, for somehow their faces had the appearance of a man.[107] He says that on other occasions he saw some in Guinea on the coast of Manegueta.[108] He says that this night, in the name of Our Lord, he will set out on his voyage, without delaying longer for anything, since he had found what he had been seeking, because he did not wish to have further controversy with that Martin Alonso, until their Highnesses learned the news of his voyage and what he had accomplished: "And afterwards," he says, "I will not endure the acts of evil persons and men of little virtue, who with small consideration presume to do what they will in opposition to him who did them honour."

THURSDAY, JANUARY 10th / He set out from the place where he had anchored and at sunset arrived at a river to which he gave the name *Rio de Gracia*,[109] three leagues to the south-east. He anchored at its mouth, where there is a good anchorage, on the east side. Going inside, there is a bank which has no more than two fathoms of water and is very narrow. Within, there is a good closed harbour, except that there are many shipworms. From them the caravel *Pinta*, in which was Martin Alonso, suffered great damage, for he says that he remained there trading for sixteen days, and there they bartered much gold, which was what Martin Alonso desired. When he had learned from the Indians that the admiral was on the coast of the same island of Española, and that he could not avoid him, he came to him, and it is said that he wished all his men in the ship to swear that he had only been there six days. But he said that his wickedness was a thing so notorious that it could not be concealed, and, says the admiral, he had made rules by which half the gold which was bartered or procured was for him, and when he came to leave that place, he took four Indian men and two girls by force, and the admiral ordered clothing to be given to them and had them returned to land that they might go to their homes: "This," he says, "is for the service of Your Highnesses, for these men and women are all Your Highnesses' and it is so especially in this island, as in the others. But here, where Your Highnesses already have a settlement, more honour and favour ought to be done to the people, since in this island there is so much gold and good lands and spices."

FRIDAY, JANUARY 11th / At midnight he set out from Rio de Gracia with the land breeze; he steered east as far as a cape which he called *Bel Prado*,[110] a distance of four leagues, and from there to the south-east is the mountain which he named *Monte de Plata*,[111] and he says that it is eight leagues from there. From Cape de Bel Prado, to the east by south, is the cape which he called *del Angél*,[112] distant eighteen leagues, and from this cape to Monte de Plata there is a gulf and the best and most lovely lands in the world, all fit for cultivation, high and beautiful, and they run far inland, and afterwards there is a range of mountains which stretches from east to west, very large and very lovely, and at the foot of the mountain there is a very good harbour, and at the entrance there are fourteen fathoms. This mountain is very high and lovely, and all is very populous, and the admiral believed that there must be good rivers and much gold. From Cape del Angél to the east by south it is four leagues to a headland which he called *del Hierro*,[113] and four leagues in the same direction there is a headland which he called *Punta Seca*,[114] and six leagues from there in the same direction is the cape which he called *Redondo*,[115] and from there to the east is Cape Francés,[116] and at this cape, on the east side, there is a large bay, but it did not seem to have anchorage. A league from there is Cape del Buen Tiempo:[117] from this to the south by east, there is a cape which he called *Tajado*,[118] at a full league's distance. From this towards the south he saw another cape, and it seemed to be fifteen leagues away. To-day he went a great distance, as the wind and currents were with him. He did not dare to anchor for fear of the shallows; and so he jogged off and on all night.

SATURDAY, JANUARY 12th / At the quarter of dawn he steered to the east with a fresh wind, and so went until day, and in this time he made twenty miles, and in the following two hours twenty-four miles. From there he saw land to the south, and went towards it; it was forty-eight miles away and he says that, keeping out to sea, he went this night twenty-eight miles to the north-north-east. When he saw the land, he named a cape, which he sighted, *Cape de Padre y Hijo*,[119] because at its point, on the east side, there were two projections, one being greater than the other. Afterwards to the east, at two leagues, he saw a great and very lovely opening between two large mountains, and he saw that it was a very large harbour, good and with a very good entrance, but because it was very early in the morning and in order not to delay his journey, for during most of the time it blows there from the east and so carries a ship north-north-west, he would not wait longer. He followed his course to the east as far as a very high and very beautiful cape, all of jagged rock, to which he gave the name *Cape del Enamo-rado*;[120] it was to the east of that harbour, which he called *Puerto Sacro*, thirty-two miles distant. When he reached it, he discovered another cape, much more lovely and much higher and rounded, all of rock,

like Cape St. Vincent in Portugal; it was twelve miles east of Cape
del Enamorado. After he had come abreast of Cape del Enamorado,
he saw between it and the other cape a very large bay, which had a
breadth of three leagues, and in the middle of it a tiny islet.[121] The
depth is great at the entrance near the land; he anchored there in twelve
fathoms. He sent the boat to land for water and to see if they could
have speech, but the people all fled. He also anchored in order to see
if all that land was one with Española and if what he called a gulf
did not form a separate island. He was amazed that the island of
Española was so large.

SUNDAY, JANUARY 13th / He did not go out of this harbour because
there was no land breeze with which to do so. He was anxious to leave
it in order to go to another better harbour, since that was somewhat
exposed and because he wished to observe the conjunction of the moon
with the sun, which he expected on the seventeenth, and the moon in
opposition with Jupiter and in conjunction with Mercury, and the sun
in opposition to Jupiter, which is the cause of great winds. He sent
the boat to land at a beautiful beach, in order that they might take
ajes to eat, and they found some men with bows and arrows, with
whom they paused to talk, and they bought two bows and many
arrows, and asked one of them to go to speak with the admiral in the
caravel, and he came. The admiral says that he was more ugly in
appearance than any whom he had seen. He had his face all stained
with charcoal, although in all other parts they are accustomed to paint
themselves with various colours; he wore all his hair very long and
drawn back and tied behind, and then gathered in meshes of parrots'
feathers, and he was as naked as the others. The admiral judged that
he must be one of the Caribs who eat men and that the gulf, which
he had seen yesterday, divided the land and that it must be an island
by itself. He questioned him concerning the Caribs, and the Indian
indicated to him that they were near there to the east, and the admiral
says that he sighted this land yesterday before he entered that bay.
The Indian told him that in that land there was much gold, and point-
ing to the poop of the caravel, which was very large, said that there
were pieces of that size. He called gold "tuob," and did not understand

Man-eating Indians; a sixteenth century woodcut.

it by "caona," as they call it in the first part of the island, or by
"nozay," as they name it in San Salvador and in the other islands.
In Española they call copper or gold of poor quality "tuob." Of the
island of Matinino, [122] the Indian said that it was entirely peopled by
women without men, and that in it there is very much "tuob," which
is gold or copper, and that it is farther to the east of Carib. He spoke
also of the island of "Goanín," where there is much "tuob." Of these
islands, the admiral says that he had been told some days before by
many persons. The admiral says further that in the islands which he
had passed they were in great terror of Carib: in some islands they
call it "Caniba," but in Española "Carib"; and they must be a daring
people, since they go through all the islands and eat the people they
can take. He says that he understood some words, and from them he
says that he gathered other things, and the Indians whom he carried
with him understood more, although they found a difference of
languages, owing to the great distance between the lands. He ordered
food to be given to the Indian, and gave him pieces of green and red

cloth, and glass beads, to which they are very much attached, and sent him back to shore. And he told him to bring him gold, if there was any, which he believed to be the case from certain small ornaments which he was wearing. When the boat reached the shore, there were behind the trees quite fifty-five men, naked, with very long hair, as women wear their hair in Castile. At the back of the head, they wore tufts of parrot feathers and feathers of other birds, and each one carried his bow. The Indian landed and caused the others to lay aside their bows and arrows and a short stick, which is like a very heavy . . . and which they carry in place of a sword.[123] Afterwards they came to the boat and the people from the boat landed, and they began to buy from them their bows and arrows and other weapons, because the admiral had ordered this to be done. When two bows had been sold, they would not give more, but prepared rather to assault the Christians and capture them. They went running to collect their bows and arrows, where they had laid them aside, and came back with ropes in their hands, in order, as he says, to bind the Christians. Seeing them come running towards them, the Christians, being on guard, as the admiral always advised them to be, fell upon them, and they gave an Indian a great slash on the buttocks and they wounded another in the breast with an arrow. When they saw that they could gain little, although the Christians were not more than seven and they were fifty and more, they turned in flight, so that not one remained, one leaving his arrows here and another his bow there. The Christians, as he says, would have killed many of them, if the pilot who went with them as their captain had not prevented it. Afterwards the Christians returned to the caravel with their boat, and when the admiral learned of it, he said that on the one hand he was sorry, and on the other hand not, since they would be afraid of the Christians, for without doubt, he says, the people there are, as he says, evil-doers, and he believed that they were those from Carib and that they eat men; accordingly, if the boat which he had left with the thirty-nine men in the fortress and town of La Navidad should come there, these would be afraid to do any ill to them. And he says that if they were not Caribs, at least they must be neighbours of them and have the same customs, and they are a fearless people, not like the others of the other islands, who are

Canibalium

Cannibals attacking Spanish ships; detail of an engraving of 1621.

cowardly beyond reason and without weapons. All this the admiral says, and that he wished to take some of them. He says that they made many smoke signals, as they were accustomed to do in that island of Española.

MONDAY, JANUARY 14th / He wished to send this night to look for the houses of those Indians, in order to take some of them, believing that they were Caribs, and owing to the strong east and north-east wind and to the high sea running, he did not do so. But as soon as it was day, they saw many Indians on land, and the admiral therefore ordered the boat to go there with people well equipped. And immediately they saw them, they all came to the stern of the boat and especially the Indian who had come to the caravel the day before and to whom the admiral had given some articles of barter. He says that with him there came a king, who had given some beads to the said Indian to present to those in the boat, as a sign of security and peace. This king, with three of his people, entered the boat and came to the caravel, and the admiral ordered that they should be given biscuit and honey to eat, and he gave him a red cap and beads and a piece of red cloth, and to the others he gave also pieces of cloth. The king said that next day he would bring a gold mask, declaring that there was much there and in Carib and Matinino. Afterwards, he sent them to land well pleased. The admiral says further that the caravels were leaking much at the keel, and he complains greatly of the caulkers who at Palos caulked them very badly, and when they saw that the admiral had noticed the poorness of their work and that he wished to make them put it right, they fled. But, despite the fact that the caravels were making much water, he trusted that our Lord, who brought him there, in His pity and mercy would lead him back, for His High Majesty well knew how much controversy he had experienced before he was able to set out from Castile, and that no other had been in his favour save Him alone because He knew his heart, and after God, their Highnesses; and all the others had been contrary to him without any reason. And he says further as follows: "And they have been the cause that the royal crown of Your Highnesses has not a hundred millions more revenue than it has, since the time that I came to serve you, which is now seven years ago the twentieth day of January, this present month, plus the accumulation which would result from now on; but the mighty God will make all well." These are his words.

TUESDAY, JANUARY 15th / He says that he wished to depart, because now there was no profit in remaining, owing to those disagreements which had occurred; he must mean the dispute with the Indians. He says also that to-day he has learned that all the abundance of gold was in the district of the town of La Navidad of their Highnesses, and that in the island of Carib and in Matinino there is much copper, although there would be difficulties in Carib, because that people is said to eat human flesh. Their island was in sight from there, and he was resolved to go to it, as it was on his course, and to the island of Matinino, which is said to be entirely peopled by women without men, and to see both and to take some of them, as he says. The admiral sent the boat ashore

and the king of that land had not come, because, he says, the village
was distant, but he sent his gold crown, as he had promised. And
there came many other men with cotton and bread and *ajes*, all with
their bows and arrows. After all had been bartered, there came, as he
says, four young men to the caravel, and they seemed to the admiral
to give so good a description of all those islands which were towards
the east on the same course, which the admiral had to take, that he
decided to carry them to Castile with him. There he says that they
have no iron nor has he seen any other metal, although in a few days it
is impossible to learn much concerning a country, owing to the
difficulty of the language, which the admiral only understood by
guesswork, and because they did not understand what he asked of
them in a few days. The bows of that people, as he says, were as large
as those of France and England; the arrows are like the spears of the
other peoples which he had visited previously, for they are of the stalks
of canes, when they are seeding, which are very straight and a yard and
a half and two yards in length, and afterwards they fix at the end a
piece of sharp wood, a palm and a half long, and into this piece of
wood some insert a fish tooth and some, the majority, put poison
there. They do not shoot them as in other parts, but in a peculiar manner so that they cannot do much harm. There was there much cotton,
very fine and long, and there is much mastic, and it seemed to him
that their bows were of yew, and that there was gold and copper.
There is also much *axi*, which is their pepper, which is worth more
than pepper, and all those people eat nothing without it, for they find
it very healthy. Fifty caravels could be loaded with it every year in
that Española. He says that he found much seaweed in that bay, of
the kind which they had found in the gulf when he came to the
discovery, on which account he believed that there were islands lying
directly to the east, from the point where he began to find them, since
he regards it as certain that this weed grows in shallow water near land,
and he says that, if this be so, these Indies were very near the Canary
Islands, and for this reason he believed that they were less than four
hundred leagues distant.

WEDNESDAY, JANUARY 16th / He set out from the gulf, which he called *Golfo de las Flechas*,[124] three hours before day with a land breeze,
and afterwards with a west wind, steering to the east by north, in order
to go, as he says, to the island of Carib, where lived the people of whom
all those islands and lands were in so great fear, because it is said that
with their innumerable canoes they go about all those seas and it is
said that they eat the men whom they can take. He says that some
Indians, of the four whom he had taken yesterday in the harbour of
las Flechas, had shown him the course. After having gone, in his
opinion, sixty-four miles, the Indians indicated to him that the island
lay to the south-east. He wished to take that route, and ordered the sails
trimmed, and after having gone two leagues, the wind became stronger, very good for going to Spain. He observed among the people that
they began to grow sad because they were turning aside from the direct
course, owing to the fact that both caravels were making much water,
and that they had no remedy save in God. He was forced to abandon
the course which he believed led to the island, and he went about to the
direct course for Spain, north-east by east, and so went forty-eight
miles, which are twelve leagues, until sunset. The Indians told him
that by that route he would find the island of Matinino, which is said
to be peopled by women without men, and which the admiral greatly
desired to visit, in order, as he says, to take to the Sovereigns five or six
of them. But he doubted whether the Indians knew the course well,
and he could not delay on account of the danger from the water which
the caravels were shipping. But he says that it was certain that there
were these women, and that at a certain time of the year men came to
them from the island of Carib, which he says was ten or twelve leagues
from them. And if they gave birth to a boy, they sent him to the island
of the men, and if to a girl, they kept her with them. The admiral
says that both islands cannot be over fifteen or twenty leagues from
where he had set out, and he believed that they were to the south-east
and that the Indians did not know how to indicate the direction to
him. After having lost sight of the cape on the island of Española
which he called *Cape de Sant Teramo*,[125] which lay sixteen leagues
to his west, he went twelve leagues to the east by north. He had very
good weather.

A caravel; in *Libre de cōsolat tractat dels fets maritims*, 1502.

THURSDAY, JANUARY 17th / Yesterday at sunset the wind fell some-what. He went on for fourteen sand glasses, each of which marks one half hour, or a little less, until the passing of the first quarter, and he made four miles an hour, that is, twenty-eight miles. Afterwards, the wind became fresher, and so he went all that quarter, which makes ten half hour glasses, and afterwards for another six, until sunset, at eight miles an hour; and so he made in all eighty-four miles, which are twenty-one leagues, to the north-east by east, and up to sunset, he made a further forty-four miles, which are eleven leagues, to the east. A booby came to the caravel, and afterwards another, and he saw much weed of the kind that is in the sea.

FRIDAY, JANUARY 18th / This night he navigated with little wind to the east by south, forty miles, which are ten leagues, and afterwards thirty miles, which are seven and a half leagues, to the south-east by east, until sunset. After sunset, he navigated all day with little wind east-north-east and north-east, and to the east, more or less, turning her prow sometimes to the north and sometimes to the north by east and north-north-east, and so, taking it all in all, he believed that he may have made sixty miles, which are fifteen leagues. Little vegetation appeared in the sea, but he says that yesterday and to-day the sea seemed to be choked with tunny-fish, and the admiral believed that from there they must go to the duke's fisheries at Conil and to the Cadiz fisheries. [126] On account of a fish called *rabiforcado*, [127] which followed in the wake of the caravel and afterwards went in the direction of the south south-east, the admiral believed that there must be some islands there, and he said that to the east-south-east of the island of Española lay the island of Carib and that of Matinino and many others.

SATURDAY, JANUARY 19th / This night he went fifty-six miles to the north by east, and sixty-four to the north-east by north. After sunset, he navigated to the north-east with the wind east-south-east, with a fresh wind, and afterwards to the north-east by north, and he went eighty-four miles, which are twenty-one leagues. He saw the sea thick with small tunny-fish; there were boobies, tropic-birds and frigate-birds.

Indian woman and platan; in Ramusio's *Navigationi et Viaggi*, 1606.

SUNDAY, JANUARY 20th / This night the wind dropped and at intervals
there were some gusts of wind, and he went in all twenty miles to the
north-east. After sunrise he went eleven miles to the south-east;
afterwards to the north-north-east thirty-six miles, which are nine

leagues. He saw innumerable small tunny-fish; he says that the breezes were very soft and sweet, as in Seville in April or May; and "The sea," he says, "was always very smooth, many thanks be given to God." Frigate-birds and petrels and many other birds were seen.

MONDAY, JANUARY 21st / Yesterday, after sunset, he navigated to the north by east, with an east and north-east wind. He went eight miles an hour until midnight, which will be fifty-six miles. Afterwards he went to the north-north-east at eight miles an hour, and so in the whole night it came to a hundred and four miles, which are twenty-six leagues, towards the north-east by north. After sunrise, he steered to the north-north-east with the same east wind, and at times to the north by east, and he went eighty-eight miles in the eleven hours of daylight, that is, twenty-one leagues, deducting one which he lost, because he fell off towards the caravel *Pinta* in order to speak with her. He found the breezes very cold, and he thought, as he says, that he would find them more so every day, as he arrived farther to the north, and also on account of the nights being longer owing to the narrowness of the sphere. Many tropic-birds and petrels and other birds were seen, but not so many fish, owing, as he says, to the water being colder. He saw much weed.

TUESDAY, JANUARY 22nd / Yesterday, after sunset, he navigated to the north-north-east with an east wind which veered to the south-east; he made eight miles an hour, until five half-hour glasses had passed and three before watch was begun, which comes to eight half-hour glasses; and so he may have gone seventy-two miles, which makes eighteen leagues. Afterwards he went to the north by east for six half-hour glasses, which will be another eighteen miles; after that, for the four half-hour glasses of the second watch to the north-east, at six miles an hour, which comes to three leagues to the north-east; afterwards, until sunrise, he went to the east-north-east for eleven half-hour glasses, six leagues an hour, which makes seven leagues; after that, to the east-north-east, until eleven o'clock, thirty-two miles; and so the wind fell, and he went no farther that day. The Indians went swimming; they saw tropic-brids and much weed.[128]

The arms of Columbus; in his *Book of Privileges*, Genoa.

WEDNESDAY, JANUARY 23rd / This night he found many variations in the winds. Being on the watch for everything and giving the attention which good seamen are accustomed and ought to give, he says that he went that night to the north-east by north eighty-four miles, which are twenty-one leagues. He waited many times for the caravel *Pinta*, because she went badly close-hauled, since she found little help from the mizzen, owing to the mast not being good; and he says that if her captain, who is Martin Alonso Pinzón, had taken as much care in the Indies to provide himself with a good mast, where there are so many and of such a kind, as he had been zealous to part company with him, thinking to stuff the ship full of gold, he would have done well. Many tern were seen and much weed; the sky was all overcast during these days, but it has not rained, and the sea has always been as smooth as a river, "Many thanks be given to God." After sunset, he went due north-east for thirty miles, which are seven leagues and a half, for some part of the day, and afterwards for the rest he went to the east-north-east a further thirty miles, which are seven leagues and a half.

THURSDAY, JANUARY 24th / He went all this night, taking into account the many variations which there were in the wind, to the north-east forty-four miles, that is, eleven leagues. After sunrise until sunset, he went to the east-north-east fourteen leagues.

FRIDAY, JANUARY 25th / He steered this night to the east-north-east for a part of the night, which was thirteen half-hour glasses, for nine leagues and a half; afterwards he went to the north-north-east another six miles. From sunrise, during the whole day, because the wind fell, he went to the east-north-east twenty-eight miles, which are seven leagues. The sailors killed a dolphin and a very large shark, and he says that they had much need of them, because they had now nothing to eat except bread and wine and *ajes* from the Indies.

SATURDAY, JANUARY 26th / This night he went to the east by south, for fifty-six miles, that is, fourteen leagues. After sunrise, he steered sometimes to the east-south-east and sometimes to the south-east. Up to

A fifteenth century astrolabe.

and then went close to the wind, and by night he went towards the north twenty-four miles, which are six leagues.

SUNDAY, JANUARY 27th / Yesterday, after sunset, he went to the northeast and north by east, and made five miles an hour, and in thirteen eleven o'clock he went forty miles; after that, he made another tack hours sixty-five miles, which are sixteen leagues and a half; after sun-rise, he went towards the north-east twenty-four miles, which are six leagues, up to midday, and from that time, until sunset, he went three leagues to the east-north-east.

MONDAY, JANUARY 28th / All this night he steered east-north-east; he made thirty-six miles, which are nine leagues. After sunrise, he went until sunset, to the east-north-east, twenty miles, which are five leagues. The breezes he found to be temperate and sweet; he saw tropic-birds and petrels and much weed.

TUESDAY, JANUARY 29th / He steered to the east-north-east, and went in the night, with a south and south-west wind, thirty-nine miles, which are nine leagues and a half; in the whole day, he made eight leagues. The breezes were very temperate as in April in Castile; the sea very smooth. Fish, which they call dorados, came to the side.

WEDNESDAY, JANUARY 30th / All this night he made seven leagues to the east-north-east. During the day, he ran to the south by east, for thirteen leagues and a half. He saw tropic-birds and much weed and many dolphins.

THURSDAY, JANUARY 31st / He steered this night to the north by east, for thirty miles, and afterwards to the north-east for thirty-five miles, which are sixteen leagues. After sunrise, until night, he went for thirteen leagues and a half to the east-north-east. They saw tropic-birds and petrels.

FRIDAY, FEBRUARY 1st / He went this night to the east-north-east, for sixteen leagues and a half. During the day he ran on the same course for twenty-nine leagues and a quarter. The sea was very smooth, thanks be to God.

SATURDAY, FEBRUARY 2nd / This night he went to the east-north-east forty miles, which are ten leagues. In the day, with the same wind astern, he ran seven miles an hour; so that in eleven hours he made seventy-seven miles, which are nineteen leagues and a quarter. The sea was very smooth, thanks to God, and the breezes very soft. They saw the sea so choked with weed that, if they had not seen it, they would have feared shoals. They saw petrels.

Columbus at sea; an engraving by Theodore de Bry.

SUNDAY, FEBRUARY 3rd / This night, the wind being astern with the sea very smooth, thanks to God, they went twenty-nine leagues. The north star appeared very high, as at Cape St. Vincent; he could not take its altitude with the astrolabe or quadrant, as the roll did not permit it. In the day he steered on his course to the east-north-east, and he made ten miles an hour, and so in eleven hours twenty-seven leagues.

MONDAY, FEBRUARY 4th / This night he steered east by north; for some part of it, he made twelve miles an hour, and for some part, ten. So he made one hundred and thirty miles, which are thirty-two leagues and a half. The sky was very overcast and rainy, and it was somewhat cold, on which account he says that he knew that he had not arrived at the islands of the Azores. After the sun had risen, he changed his course, and went to the east; he went in the whole day seventy-seven miles, which are nineteen leagues and a quarter.

TUESDAY, FEBRUARY 5th / This night he steered east; in the whole of it, he went fifty-four miles, which are fourteen leagues, less a half. During the day he ran ten miles an hour, and so in eleven hours they went one hundred and ten miles, which are twenty-seven leagues and a half. They saw petrels and some small sticks, which was a sign that they were near land.

WEDNESDAY, FEBRUARY 6th / This night he navigated to the east; he made eleven miles an hour in thirteen hours of the night; he went one hundred and forty-three miles, which are thirty-five leagues and a quarter. They saw many birds and petrels. During the day he ran fourteen miles an hour, and so on that day he went one hundred and fifty-four miles, which are thirty-eight leagues and a half, so that, day and night together, they went seventy-four leagues, a little more or less. Vincente Yañez found that to-day in the morning the island of Flores lay to his north and the island of Madeira to the east. [129] Roldán said that the island of Fayal or that of San Gregorio lay to the north-north-east, and Porto Santo to the east. [130] Much weed was seen.

THURSDAY, FEBRUARY 7th / He navigated this night to the east; he made ten miles an hour, and so in thirteen hours one hundred and thirty miles, which are thirty-two leagues and a half; during the day, he made eight miles an hour; in eleven hours he made eighty-eight miles, which are twenty-two leagues. On this morning the admiral was seventy-five leagues to the south of the island of Flores, and the pilot Pero Alonso,[131] steering north, passed between Tercera and the island of Santa Maria, and steering east, passed to the windward of the island of Madeira, twelve leagues to the northward. The sailors saw weed of a different kind from that previously seen, and of which there is much in the islands of the Azores; afterwards, they saw the same kind as before.

FRIDAY, FEBRUARY 8th / He went this night three miles an hour to the east for a while, and afterwards he steered east by south. In the whole night he made twelve leagues. From sunrise to midday he ran twenty-seven miles; afterwards, until sunset, he ran as many more, that is thirteen leagues to the south-south-east.

SATURDAY, FEBRUARY 9th / During part of the night he went three leagues to the south-south-east, and afterwards to the south by east. Afterwards, he went to the north-east, until ten o'clock, for a further five leagues, and then, until night, he went nine leagues to the east.

SUNDAY, FEBRUARY 10th / After sunset, he steered east all night for one hundred and thirty miles, which are thirty-two leagues and a half; the sun having risen, he went nine miles an hour until night, and so in eleven hours he made ninety-nine miles more, which are twenty-four leagues and three-quarters. In the caravel of the admiral, Vincente Yañez and the two pilots, Sancho Ruiz[132] and Pero Alonso Niño, and Roldán, charted their course or fixed their position. They all made it much beyond the islands of the Azores to the east according to their charts, and navigating to the north, no one touched the island of Santa Maria, which is the last of all the islands of the Azores, but rather they would be five leagues beyond it and in the neighbourhood of the island of Madeira or in that of Porto Santo. But the admiral found himself much out of his course, making his position very far behind theirs. This night the island of Flores lay to his north, and to the east he was going in the direction of Nafe in Africa,[133] and passed to the windward of the island of Madeira, . . . leagues to the north.

They thus made themselves a hundred and fifty leagues nearer Castile than he did. He says that, by the grace of God, when they see land, it will be known who took their position the more accurately. He says here that he went two hundred and sixty-three leagues beyond the island of Hierro, on the outward voyage, before he saw the first weed, etc.

MONDAY, FEBRUARY 11th / He went this night twelve miles an hour on his course, and so in the whole night he reckoned thirty-nine leagues, and in the whole day he ran sixteen leagues and a half. He saw many birds, on account of which he believed that he was near land.

TUESDAY, FEBRUARY 12th / He navigated to the east at six miles an hour this night, and by daybreak he went seventy-three miles, which are eighteen leagues and a quarter. Here he began to experience heavy seas and stormy weather, and he says if the caravel had not been very good and well equipped, he would have feared to be lost. During the day he ran eleven or twelve leagues with great toil and danger.

WEDNESDAY, FEBRUARY 13th / After sunset, until day, he experienced great difficulty from the wind and from the very high sea, and the stormy weather. It flashed with lightning three times to the north-north-east; he said that this was an indication of a great storm which would come from that direction or against him. For most of the night, he went with bare poles; afterwards he hoisted a little sail and went fifty-two miles, which are thirteen leagues. This day the wind moderated a little, but presently it increased, and the sea became terrible, and the waves met each other, so that they strained the ships. He made fifty-five miles, which are thirteen leagues and a half.

THURSDAY, FEBRUARY 14th / This night the wind increased and the waves were terrible, one meeting another, so that they crossed and held back the ship, which could not go forward or come out from the midst of them, and they broke over her. He carried the mainsail very low, merely in order to escape to some extent from the waves; he so went for three hours and ran twenty miles. The sea and wind increased much, and, seeing that the danger was great, he began to

ℭ𝔇emonſtracion de los vientos.

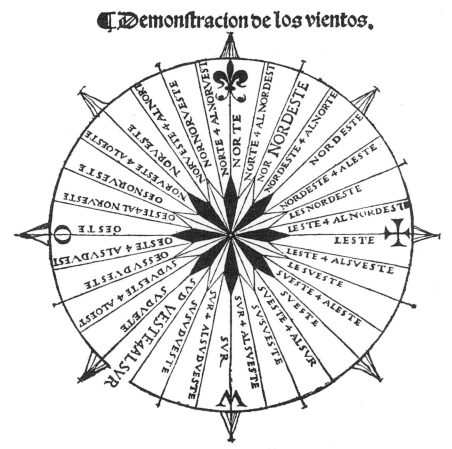

A wind rose; in Cortes' *Breve compendio de la sphera y del arte de navegar*, 1551.

run before the wind where it bore him, as there was no other recourse. Then the caravel *Pinta*, in which was Martin Alonso, also began to run before the wind and disappeared, although all night the admiral made flares and the other vessel answered, until, as it seems, she could do so no more owing to the violence of the storm and because she was very far out of the course of the admiral. This night the admiral went to the north-east by east fifty-four miles, which are thirteen leagues. The sun having risen, the wind and sea were greater, the cross waves more terrible. He set only the mainsail and carried it low, in order that the ship might get out from among the waves which crossed, and threatened to sink her. He followed the course to the east-north-east, and afterwards, to the east by north. He so went for six hours, and in them made seven leagues and a half. He ordered a pilgrimage to be vowed, that some one should go to Santa Maria de Guadalupe[134] and carry a wax candle of five pounds, and that all should vow that he, upon whom the lot should fall, should perform the pilgrimage. For this purpose, he commanded as many chick-peas to be taken as there were persons in the ship, and that one should be marked with a knife, making a cross, and that they should be placed in a cap and well shaken. The first to put in his hand was the admiral, and he drew out the pea marked with the cross, and so the lot fell upon him, and from that moment he regarded himself as a pilgrim and as bound to go to fulfil the vow. Lots were cast again to send a pilgrim to Santa Maria de Loreto, which is in the March of Ancona, the land of the pope, and which is the house where Our Lady has done and does many and great miracles, and the lot fell upon a sailor from Puerto de Santa Maria, who was called Pedro de Villa, and the admiral promised to give him money for his expenses. He decided that another pilgrim should be sent to watch for one night at Santa Clara de Moguer and cause a mass to be said, and for this purpose they once more used the chick-peas, and that marked with the cross, and the lot fell on the admiral himself. After this, the admiral and all the people made a vow that, on reaching the first land, they would all go in their shirts in procession to pray in a church dedicated to Our Lady. Besides the general vows or those made in common, each one made his own individual vow, because no one expected to escape, all regarding themselves as lost, owing to the terrible storm which they were experiencing. It contributed to increase the danger that the ship was short of ballast, as the cargo had been lightened, the stores of food having been already eaten and the water and wine drunk; owing to his eager desire to avail himself of the fine weather which they experienced among the islands, the admiral did not provide ballast, intending to have it taken in at the island of the women, where he proposed to go. The remedy which he found for this need was, when they were able to do so, to fill the casks full with sea water, they being empty of water and wine,

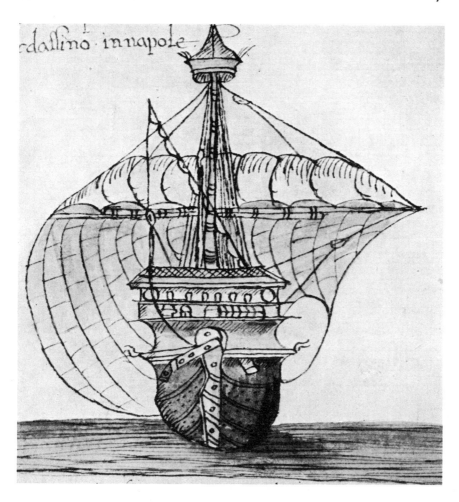

and in this way they supplied that need. Here the admiral writes of the reasons which caused him to fear that Our Lord willed that he should perish there, and of other reasons which gave him hope that God would bring him in safety, so that such news, as he was bearing to the Sovereigns, should not be lost. It seemed to him that the great desire which he had to bring this momentous news and to show that he had been proved a truth-teller in what he had said and had offered to discover, inspired him with the greatest fear that he would

not achieve this, and he says that he feared that the most trifling
annoyance might interrupt and prevent it. He assigns this to his little
faith and to his lack of confidence in the divine providence; on the
other hand, he drew comfort from the blessings which God had shown
to him in giving him so great a victory, in the discovery of what he
had discovered, and God had fulfilled all his desires, after he had
experienced many adversities and much opposition in Castile at his
setting out; and as in the past he committed his fate and entrusted all
his undertaking to God, and He had heard him and had given him
all that he sought, so he must believe that He would finish what had
been begun and bring him to safety, more especially because on his
outward journey, when he had greater reason to fear, God had delivered
him from the difficulties which he had with the sailors and with the
people whom he had with him, all of whom with one voice were
resolved to rise against him and return, making protests; and the
everlasting God had given him strength and courage against them
all, and there were other things of great wonder which God had shown
forth in him and for him on that voyage, beyond those things which
their Highnesses knew from the members of their household. So that
he says that he should not have feared the said storm; "But his weak-
ness and anxiety," he says, "did not permit his mind to be soothed."
He says further that he felt also great anxiety for two sons whom he
had in Cordoba at school, for he would leave them orphaned of father
and mother in a strange land,[135] and that the Sovereigns would not
know the services which he had rendered to them on that voyage and
the most favourable news which he was bearing to them, so that they
might be moved to succour his sons. For this reason, and that their
Highnesses might know how Our Lord had given him the victory in
all that he desired in the matter of the Indies, and that it might be
known that in those parts there is no storm, which, he says, may be
gathered from the grass and trees which take root and grow almost
into the sea, and that, if he were lost in that tempest, the Sovereigns
might have news of his voyage, he took a parchment and wrote on
it all that he could about all the things he had found, earnestly begging
whomsoever might find it to carry it to the Sovereigns. This parchment he enclosed in a waxed cloth, very carefully fastened, and he

View of Genoa; in Schedel's *Liber Chronicarum*, 1493.

commanded a large wooden barrel to be brought, and placed it in it, without any one knowing what it was, for they thought that it was some act of devotion, and he ordered it thrown into the sea. Afterwards, with showers and storms, the wind changed to the west, and he went before it with only the foresail set for five hours, the sea being very rough, and he made two leagues and a half to the northeast. He had taken down the square sail from the mainmast, fearing that some wave from the sea might carry it away.

FRIDAY, FEBRUARY 15th / Yesterday, after sunset, the sky began to clear towards the west, and showed that it was about to blow from very high, although it was lessening a little. He went to the east-north-that quarter. He added the bonnet to the mainsail. The sea was still east at four miles an hour, and in thirteen hours of night they went thirteen leagues. After sunrise, they sighted land, which showed itself ahead of them to the east-north-east; some said that it was the island of Madeira, others that it was the rock of Cintra, in Portugal, near Lisbon. Presently the wind changed to a head wind from the east-north-east, and the sea to the west became very high; the caravel was about five leagues from land. The admiral, according to his navigation, found that he was off the islands of the Azores, and he believed that land to be one of them; the pilots and sailors found themselves already off the coast of Castile.

SATURDAY, FEBRUARY 16th / He beat against the wind all this night in order to reach land, which he already realised was an island. At times he went to the north-east, at others to the north-north-east, until sunrise, when he steered southward in order to arrive at the island, which they now could no longer see owing to the very cloudy weather. He saw astern another island at a distance of eight leagues. After sunrise until night, he continued making attempts to reach land, there being a high wind and a heavy sea. At the saying of the *Salve*, which is at the beginning of the night, some saw a light to the leeward, and it seemed that it must be the island which they saw first yesterday, and all night he was beating about and drawing as near to it as he could, to find whether at sunrise he would sight some of the islands. This night the admiral took some rest, for since Wednesday he had not slept nor been able to sleep, and he was very crippled in his legs, owing to having been constantly exposed to the cold and water, and owing to the small amount that he had eaten. At sunrise, he steered to the south-south-west, and at night he reached the island, and owing to the heavy clouds he could not recognise what island it was.

MONDAY, FEBRUARY 18th / Yesterday, after sunset, he went on, rounding the island, in order to find where he might anchor and have speech; he cast anchor with an anchor which he lost at once; he sailed on once more and beat about all night. After sunrise, he again reached the northern side of the island, anchored where it looked best, and sent the boat ashore, and they had speech with the people of the island, and they learned that it was the island of Santa Maria, one of those

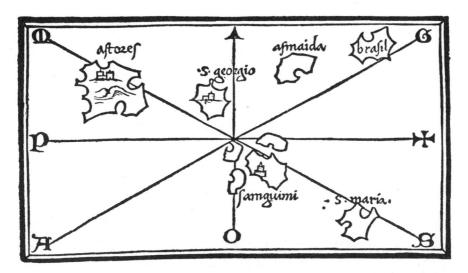

The Azores; in Bordone's *Isolario*, 1528.

of the Azores, and the inhabitants indicated to them a harbour where they should bring the caravel. The people of the island said that they had never seen such a storm as that which there had been for the last fifteen days, and they marvelled how they had escaped. He says that they gave many thanks to God and rejoiced greatly upon learning that the admiral had discovered the Indies. The admiral says that this navigation of his had been very sure and that he had charted his course well, for which many thanks should be given to Our Lord, although he had made it a little farther on; but he had been certain that he was in the neighbourhood of the Azores, and that this island was one of them. And he says that he pretended to have gone a greater distance in order to confound the pilots and sailors who did the charts, that he might remain master of that route to the Indies, as in fact he did remain, for no one of all those was certain of his course, with the result that no one could be sure of the route to the Indies.

TUESDAY, FEBRUARY 19th / After sunset, there came to the shore three men of the island and called. He sent the boat to them and they came in it, and brought fowls and fresh bread, and it was Carnival Day, and they brought other things sent by the captain of the island, who

was called Juan de Castañeda,[136] who sent word that he knew him very
well, and that, as it was night, he did not come to see him, but would
come at daybreak and bring more refreshment, and he would bring
with him three men from the caravel who remained there, whom he
had not sent on account of the great pleasure which he had with them,
in hearing the details of the voyage. The admiral ordered great honour
to be done to the messengers, commanding beds to be given to them,
in which they might sleep that night, because it was late and the
settlement was at a distance. And because on the previous Thursday,
when he found himself in the anguish of the storm, they had made
a vow and the vows mentioned above, and the vow that in the first
land where there was a house of Our Lady, they would go in their
shirts, etc., he decided that one-half of the people should go in fulfilment to a small house, which was near the sea and like a hermitage,
and that he would go afterwards with the other half. Seeing that the
land was safe and trusting in the offers of the captain and in the peace
which there was between Portugal and Castile, he asked the three men
to go to the village, and have a priest come to say mass for them. They
went in their shirts, in fulfilment of their pilgrimage, and as they were
at prayer, there fell upon them the whole village on horse and on
foot, with the captain, and made them all prisoners. Afterwards, the
admiral, being without suspicion, awaited the boat in order to go to
fulfil his pilgrimage with the remaining people. At eleven o'clock,
when he saw that they did not come, he suspected that they had been
kept or that the boat had been wrecked, because all the island is
surrounded by very high cliffs. The admiral could not see the affair,
because the hermitage was behind a point. He weighed anchor and
sailed directly towards the hermitage, and saw many men on horse-
back, who dismounted and entered the boat in arms and came to the
caravel to arrest the admiral. The captain stood up in the boat and
asked a safe conduct from the admiral. He replied that he granted it
to him, but what change was this that none of his people were in the
boat? And the admiral added that if he would come and enter the
caravel, all would be done as he desired. The admiral was trying to
draw him on board with smooth words, that he might take him and
recover his men. He did not believe that he was breaking faith by

A mariner's hour glass.

giving him a safe conduct, since the captain had offered peace and security and had not kept his word. The captain would not trust himself on board because, as he says, he had evil intentions. Having seen that he would not come to the caravel, the admiral asked him to explain why he detained his men, adding that this would offend the King of Portugal, and that in the territory of the Sovereigns of Castile the Portuguese received much honour, and entered it and were as safe as in Lisbon; and since the Sovereigns had given him letters of credence for all the princes and lords and men in the world, he would exhibit them to him, if he would come on board, and as he was their admiral of the Ocean Sea and viceroy of the Indies which now belonged to their Highnesses, he would show their provisions, signed with their signatures, and sealed with their seals, and he showed them to him at a distance. And he said that the Sovereigns were in great love and friendship with the King of Portugal, and they had commanded him to show all the honour he could to ships of Portugal which he might encounter, and supposing the captain would not give up his men to him, he would not on that account refrain from going to Castile, since he had sufficient men to navigate to Seville, and the captain and his men would be well punished for having committed this offence. Then the captain replied that he and the others did not recognise the King and Queen of Castile, or their letters, nor did they fear them; on the contrary, they would have him understand that this was Portugal, saying this in a rather threatening manner. When the admiral heard this, he was greatly concerned, and he says that he thought that some dispute must have occurred between the one kingdom and the other after his departure, and he could not refrain from making that reply to them which was proper. Afterwards, as he says, that captain again stood up at a distance and told the admiral that he should go with the caravel to the harbour and that all he was doing and had done, the King his master had sent him orders to do. The admiral called those who were in the caravel to witness this, and the admiral again called to the captain and to them all, and gave them his faith and swore that he, such as he was, would not land or leave the caravel until he had carried a hundred Portuguese to Castile and depopulated all that island. And so he returned to anchor

View of Granada; in Pedro Medina's *Libro de grandezas de España*, 1548.

in the harbour where he had first been, as the weather and wind were very unsuitable for him to do anything else.

WEDNESDAY, FEBRUARY 20th / He commanded the ship to be refitted and the casks to be filled with sea water as ballast, because he was in a very poor harbour, and he was afraid that his cables might be cut, and so it happened. On this account, he sailed towards the island of San Miguel, although in no one of the islands of the Azores is there a good harbour for such weather as there then was, and he had no recourse but to escape out to sea.

THURSDAY, FEBRUARY 21st / Yesterday he set out from that island of Santa Maria for the island of San Miguel to see if he could find a harbour in which to endure such bad weather as he was experiencing, with high wind and a heavy sea. He went on until night without being able to see land either in one direction or the other, on account of the thick clouds and darkness caused by the wind and sea. The admiral says that he was not contented, because he had only three sailors who knew the sea, since most of those who were with him knew nothing of the sea. He beat about all night in a very severe storm and in great danger and toil, and in this Our Lord showed mercy to him in that the sea or its waves came from one direction only, because, if they had crossed one another as had been the case before, he would have suffered much greater distress. After sunrise, having found that he could not see the island of San Miguel, he resolved to return to Santa Maria, to see if he could recover his people and the boat and the cables and anchors which he had left there. He says that he was amazed at the very bad weather which he experienced in those islands and in that neighbourhood, because in the Indies he navigated all that winter without dropping anchor, and had always good weather, and not for a single hour did he find the sea such as he would have been unable to navigate, and in these islands he had endured so great a tempest, and the same had befallen him on his outward voyage to the islands of the Canaries, but when he had passed them, he had found the breezes and the sea always temperate. In conclusion, the admiral says that the sacred theologians and learned philosophers were right in saying that the earthly paradise is at the end of the east, because it is a very temperate place, so those lands which he had now discovered are, he says, "the end of the east."

FRIDAY, FEBRUARY 22nd / Yesterday he anchored at the island of Santa Maria in the place or harbour where he had first anchored, and immediately there came a man who called from some rocks which were opposite that place, saying that they should not go away from there. Afterwards came the boat with five sailors and two priests and a notary; they asked for a safe conduct, and when it had been given by the admiral, they came on board the caravel and as it was night they slept there, and the admiral showed them such honour as he could. In the morning they required him to show them his commission from the Sovereigns of Castile, in order to prove to them that it was by their authority that he had made that voyage. The admiral felt that

Portrait of Isabel the Catholic by Bartolomé Bermejo.

they did this in order to make some show of not having done wrong, but of being right, because they had not been able to take the person of the admiral, whom they obviously meant to get into their hands since they came armed in the boat; but they found that the game was not turning out well for them and they feared what the admiral had said and threatened, which he intended to do and believed that he could succeed in doing. Finally, in order to recover the people whom they held, he had to show to them the circular letter of credence from the Sovereigns for all princes and lords, and other provisions, and he gave them of that which he had, and they went ashore satisfied, and afterwards released all the people with the boat, from whom he learned that if they had taken the admiral, they would never have let him go free, for the captain said that the King, his master, had so commanded him.

SATURDAY, FEBRUARY 23rd / Yesterday the weather began to improve: he weighed anchor and rounded the island to seek some good anchorage, in order to take in wood and stone for ballast, and he could not find anchorage until the hour of complines.[137]

SUNDAY, FEBRUARY 24th / Yesterday he anchored in the afternoon to take in wood and stone, and as the sea was very high, the boat could not reach the shore, and at the passing of the first watch of the night, it began to blow west and south-west. He ordered the sails to be hoisted, on account of the great danger that it is in those islands to lie at anchor with a south wind, and because when it blows from the south-west, it afterwards blows from the south. And having found that the weather was good for going to Castile, he abandoned the taking in of wood and stone, and had them steer to the east, and by sunrise, which was six hours and a half, he went seven miles an hour, which comes to forty-five miles and a half. After sunrise until sunset, he made six miles an hour, so that in eleven hours they went sixty-six miles, and with forty-five and a half in the night, they went one hundred and eleven and a half, and thus twenty-eight leagues.

MONDAY, FEBRUARY 25th / Yesterday, after sunset, he steered to the east on his course at five miles an hour; in thirteen hours of this night,

The port of Lisbon; an engraving by Theodore de Bry.

he made sixty-five miles, which are sixteen leagues and a quarter. After sunrise until sunset, he went a further sixteen leagues and a half, with a smooth sea, thanks to God. There came to the caravel a very large bird, which appeared to be an eagle.

TUESDAY, FEBRUARY 26th / Yesterday, after sunset, he navigated on his course to the east, the sea being smooth, thanks to God. During most of the night, he went eight miles an hour; he made a hundred miles, which are twenty-five leagues. After sunrise, with a light wind, he met with rain showers; he went a matter of eight leagues to the east-north-east.

WEDNESDAY, FEBRUARY 27th / This night and day he went out of his course, owing to contrary winds and heavy waves and sea, and he found himself a hundred and twenty-five leagues from Cape St. Vincent, and eighty from the island of Madeira, and a hundred and six from that of Santa Maria. He was very grieved at so great a storm when he was on the threshold of home.

THURSDAY, FEBRUARY 28th / He went in the same way for this night. With shifting winds, he went to the south, to the south-east, and to one side and the other, and then to the north-east and east-north-east, and in the same way all this day.

FRIDAY, MARCH 1st / This night he went to the east by north, for twelve leagues; during the day he ran to the east by north, for twenty-three leagues and a half.

SATURDAY, MARCH 2nd / He went on this course to the east by north, this night for twenty-eight leagues, and in the day he ran twenty leagues.

SUNDAY, MARCH 3rd / After sunset, he navigated on his course to the east. There came a squall which tore all the sails, and he saw himself in great peril; but God willed to deliver them. He cast lots to send a pilgrim, as he says, who should go in his shirt to Santa María de la Cinta in Huelva, and the lot fell on the admiral. They all also made a vow to fast on bread and water on the first Saturday after they reached land. He made sixty miles before the sails were torn; afterwards they went with bare poles, owing to the great storm of wind and sea which from two sides broke over them. They saw indications that they were near land; they found themselves to be very near Lisbon.

MONDAY, MARCH 4th / Last night they experienced a terrible storm, so that they thought that they were lost owing to the seas which came upon them from two sides, and the winds, which seemed to lift the

View of Lisbon; in Pedro Medina's *Libro de grandezas de España*, 1548.

caravel into the air, and the water from the sky and lightning from many sides. It pleased Our Lord to sustain them, and so he went until the first watch, when Our Lord showed him land, the sailors seeing it. And then, in order not to come to it until he might know it and see if he could find some harbour or place where they might be safe, he hoisted the mainsail, having no other resource, and went some way, although with great danger, keeping out to sea, and so God preserved them until day, as he says, with infinite labour and terror. When day came, he recognised the land as being the rock of Cintra, which is close to the river of Lisbon, where he resolved to enter, because he could do nothing else, so terrible was the storm which prevailed at the town of Cascaes which is at the entrance of the river.[138] He says that the people of the place were all that morning offering up prayers for them, and after he was within, the people came to see them in wonder that they had in any way escaped. And so at the hour of terce, he came to rest at Rastelo within the river of Lisbon, where he learned from the mariners that never had there been a winter with so many storms, and that twenty-five ships had been wrecked on the coast of Flanders, and that other vessels were lying there which for four months had not been able to put out to sea. The admiral wrote at once to the King of Portugal, who was nine leagues from there, that the Sovereigns of Castile had commanded him not to fail to enter the harbours of His Highness to ask for what he might need in return for payment, and he begged the King to give him permission to proceed with the caravel to the city of Lisbon, because some rogues, thinking that he was carrying much gold, might set themselves to commit some villainy against him, being in a deserted harbour, and also that the King might know that he did not come from Guinea but from the Indies.

TUESDAY, MARCH 5th / The great ship of the King of Portugal was also anchored at Rastelo;[139] she was the best equipped with cannon and arms of any ship that had ever been seen, and her master was called Bartolomé Diaz of Lisbon.[140] This master came in the armed boat to the caravel and told the admiral that he should enter the boat to go to give account to the factors of the King and to the captain of the said ship. The admiral replied that he was admiral of the Sovereigns of Castile and that he did not render accounts of such a kind to such persons, and that he would not leave the ships or vessels where he was, unless it were under compulsion of force which he could not resist. The master answered that he should send the master of the caravel. The admiral said that neither the master nor any other persons should go save by force, since he regarded it as the same thing to permit any one to go as to go himself, and that it was the custom of the admirals of the Sovereigns of Castile to die before they would yield or allow their people to yield. The master moderated his tone, and said that, since he was so determined, it should be as he wished, but he asked him to have the letters of the Sovereigns of Castile, if he had them, shown to him. The admiral was pleased to exhibit them, and the master at once returned to his ship and gave an account to her captain, who was called Alvaro Damán. He came to the caravel in great state,

Columbus with a globe showing the New World; an engraving of 1621.

with drums and trumpets and pipes, making a great display, and talked with the admiral and offered to do all that he might command him.

WEDNESDAY, MARCH 6th / When it was known to-day that the admiral came from the Indies, so many people came from the city of

Lisbon to see him and to see the Indians, that it was a thing of wonder. They all marvelled, giving thanks to Our Lord, and saying that it was owing to the great faith of the Sovereigns of Castile, and their desire to serve God, that the Divine Majesty had given them all this.

THURSDAY, MARCH 7th / To-day there came an infinite number of people to the caravel and many gentlemen, and among them the factors of the King, and they all gave infinite thanks to Our Lord for the great good and increase of Christendom which Our Lord had given to the Sovereigns of Castile, and he says that they attributed this to the fact that their Highnesses laboured and exercised themselves for the further-ance of the religion of Christ.

FRIDAY, MARCH 8th / To-day the admiral received a letter from the King of Portugal by Don Martin de Noroña,[141] in which he asked him to come to the place where he was, since the weather was not suitable for the departure of the caravel. And he did so, in order to disarm suspicion, although he did not wish to go, and he went to sleep at Sacabén.[142] The King commanded his factors that they should give without payment everything the admiral and his people and the caravel might need, and that all should be done as the admiral desired.

SATURDAY, MARCH 9th / To-day he left Sacabén to go where the King was, which was in the valley of Paraiso,[143] nine leagues from Lisbon. As it was raining, he could not reach there until night. The King commanded the chief persons of his household to receive him very honourably, and the King also received him with great honour, and showed him much favour and commanded him to be seated. He spoke very amiably, offering to command all to be done which might be of use to the Sovereigns of Castile and for their service, completely and more so than if it were for himself, and he showed that he was very pleased that there had been a successful conclusion to that voyage and that it had been accomplished, but he understood that according to the capitulation which had been made between the Sovereigns and himself, that conquest belonged to him. To this the admiral replied that he had not seen the capitulation nor did he know anything save that the Sovereigns had commanded that he should not go to La Mina[144]

Excerpt from Las Casas' manuscript of the *Journal*; Biblioteca Nacional, Madrid.

or any part of Guinea, and that so it had been proclaimed in all the ports of Andalusia before he set out on his voyage. The King graciously answered that he was sure that in this matter there would be no need for arbitrators; he handed him over as a guest to the prior of Crato, he being the most important personage who was there, [145] and from him the admiral received much honour and favour.

SUNDAY, MARCH 10th / To-day, after mass, the King repeated to him that if he had need of anything, it should be immediately given to him, and he had a long conversation with the admiral concerning his voyage, and always ordered him to be seated and did him much honour.

MONDAY, MARCH 11th / To-day he bade farewell to the King who told him certain things which he was to say to the Sovereigns on his behalf, showing him always great affection. He departed after eating, and His Highness sent with him Don Martin de Noroña, and all those cavaliers came to accompany him and to do him honour for a considerable distance. Afterwards, he came to a monastery of San Antonio, [146] which is near a place called Villafranca, where the Queen was, and he went to do her reverence and to kiss her hands, because she had sent to him to say that he was not to go away until he had seen her. With her were the duke and the marquis, [147] and there the admiral received much honour. The admiral left her at night and went to sleep at Alhandra. [148]

TUESDAY, MARCH 12th / To-day, being ready to leave Alhandra for the caravel, there came a squire of the King who offered him on his behalf that, if he wished to go to Castile by land, he would go with him to arrange for lodging and to order that beasts should be supplied and all that might be needed. When the admiral parted from him, he commanded a mule to be given to him and another to his pilot whom he had with him, and he says that the squire ordered a present of twenty espadims [149] to be made to the pilot, as the admiral learned. He says that all was reported to have been done so that the Sovereigns might know of it. He reached the caravel at night.

WEDNESDAY, MARCH 13th / To-day, at eight o'clock, at ebb tide and with a north-north-west wind, he weighed anchor and set sail to go to Seville.

THURSDAY, MARCH 14th / Yesterday, after sunset, he followed his course to the south, and before sunrise he found himself off Cape St. Vincent, which is in Portugal. Afterwards he steered to the east, to go to Saltés, and he went all day with a light wind, until now when he is off Faro.[150]

FRIDAY, MARCH 15th / Yesterday, after sunset, he went on his course until day with little wind, and at sunrise, he found himself off Saltés, and at midday, with a rising tide, he entered by the bar of Saltés into the port[151] from which he had departed on the third day of August in the previous year. And so he says that here ends this writing, save that he intended to go to Barcelona by sea, having had news that their Highnesses were in that city, and this in order to give them an account of all his voyage which Our Lord had permitted him to perform, and to which He had inspired him. For certainly, besides the fact that he knew and held firmly and surely without a trace of doubt that the Divine Majesty brings all good things to pass, and that all is good, save sin, and that nothing can be imagined or thought save with His consent, "Of this voyage," says the admiral, "I know that this has been miraculously shown to be so, as can be understood from this writing, by the many notable miracles which He has shown forth on the voyage and for me, who for so long a time was in the court of Your Highness with the opposition of so many chief persons of your household and against their opinion, for they were all against me, regarding this undertaking as a jest, and I hope in Our Lord that it will be the greatest honour for Christendom to have been brought forth so easily."

These are the last words of the admiral Don Christopher Columbus concerning his first voyage to the Indies and their discovery, and he had assuredly much reason and spoke as a very prudent man and almost as a prophet, although carnal men have not appreciated the goods which God offered to Spain, both, spiritual and temporal; but for her ambition and greed Spain was not worthy to enjoy the spiritual good, save for some servants of God.[152]

Thanks be to God.

Natives of the New World; detail of a map by P. Reinel, c. 1519.

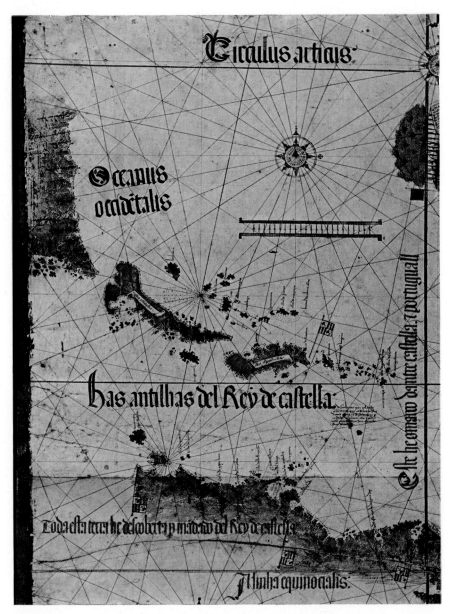

The New World; detail of the 'Cantino' world map, 1502.

Portrait of Christopher Columbus.

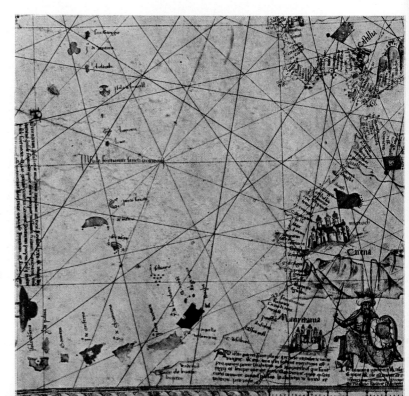

Atlantic islands; detail of a chart
by G. Benincasa, 1482.

Portuguese Carracks (detail); attributed to C. Anthoniszoon, c. 1521.

onore li le fece affay e · di
legria granme · si anday e

Caravels depicted in a fifteenth century Italian manuscript.

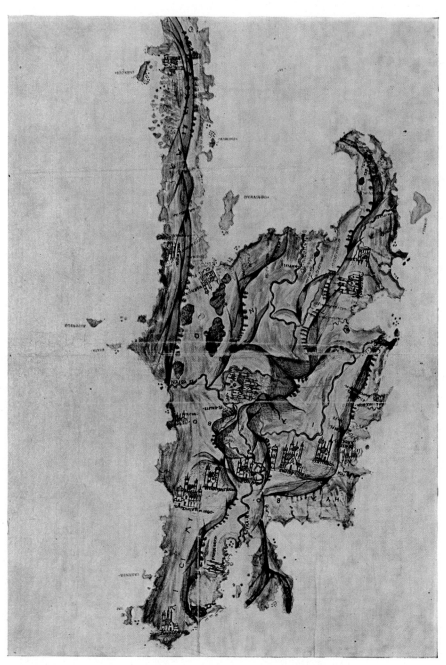

Map of San Domingo; perhaps by Bartholomew Columbus.

Parrots found in the New World;
detail of the 'Cantino' world map, 1502.

Portuguese Carracks (detail);
attributed to C. Anthoniszoon, c. 1521.

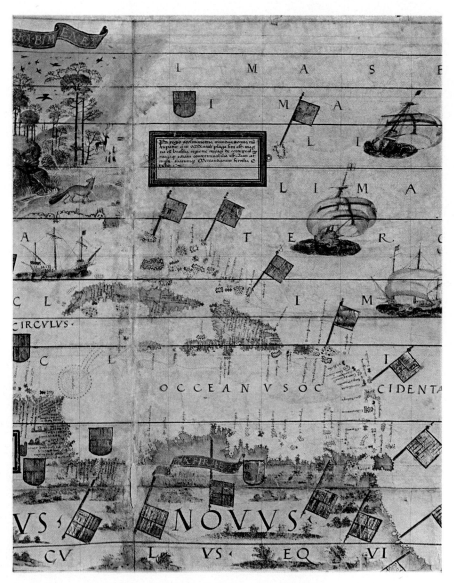

The New World; detail of a map by P. Reinel, c. 1519.

Letter of Columbus, describing the results
of his first voyage

Sᴵʀ: Since I know that you will be pleased at the great victory with which Our Lord has crowned my voyage, I write this to you, from which you will learn how in thirty-three days I passed from the Canary Islands to the Indies, with the fleet which the most illustrious King and Queen, our Sovereigns, gave to me. There I found very many islands, filled with innumerable people, and I have taken possession of them all for their Highnesses, done by proclamation and with the royal standard unfurled, and no opposition was offered to me.

To the first island which I found I gave the name "San Salvador," in remembrance of the Divine Majesty, Who had marvellously bestowed all this; the Indians call it "Guanahani." To the second, I gave the name the island of "Santa Maria de Concepcion," to the third, "Fernandina," to the fourth, "Isabella," to the fifth island, "Juana," and so each received from me a new name.

When I came to Juana, I followed its coast to the westward, and I found it to be so extensive that I thought that it must be the mainland, the province of Cathay. And since there were neither towns nor villages on the seashore, but small hamlets only, with the people of which I could not have speech because they all fled immediately, I went forward on the same course, thinking that I could not fail to find great cities or towns. At the end of many leagues, seeing that there was no change and that the coast was bearing me northwards, which I wished to avoid, since winter was already approaching and I proposed to make from it to the south, and as, moreover, the wind was carrying me forward, I determined not to wait for a change in the weather and retraced my path as far as a remarkable harbour known to me. From that point, I sent two men inland to learn if there were a king or great cities. They travelled three days' journey, finding an infinity of small hamlets and people without number, but nothing of importance. For this reason, they returned.

I understood sufficiently from other Indians, whom I had already taken, that this land was nothing but an island, and I therefore followed its coast eastward for one hundred and seven leagues to the point where it ended. From that point, I saw another island, distant about eighteen leagues from the first, to the east, and to it I at once gave the name "Española." I went there and followed its northern coast, as I had followed that of Juana, to the eastward for one hundred and eighty-eight great leagues in a straight line.[1] This island and all the others are very fertile to a limitless degree, and this island is extremely so. In it there are many harbours on the coast of the sea, beyond comparison with others that I know in Christendom, and many rivers, good and large, which is marvellous. Its lands are high; there are in it many sierras and very lofty mountains, beyond comparison with that of Tenerife. All are most beautiful, of a thousand shapes; all are accessible and are filled with trees of a thousand kinds and tall, so that they seem to touch the sky. I am told that they never lose their foliage, and this I can believe, for I saw them as green and lovely as they are in Spain in May, and some of them were flowering, some bearing fruit, and some at another stage, according to their nature. The nightingale was singing and other birds of a thousand kinds, in the month of November, there where I went. There are six or eight kinds of palm, which are a wonder to behold on account of their beautiful variety, but so are the other trees and fruits and plants. In it are marvellous pine groves; there are very wide and fertile plains, and there is honey; and there are birds of many kinds and fruits in great

A ship like the *Santa Maria*; in the illustrated edition of the Columbus letter, 1493.

diversity. In the interior, there are mines of metals, and the population is without number.

Española is a marvel. The sierras and the mountains, the plains, the champaigns, are so lovely and so rich for planting and sowing, for breeding cattle of every kind, for building towns and villages. The harbours of the sea here are such as cannot be believed to exist unless they have been seen, and so with the rivers, many and great, and of good water, the majority of which contain gold. In the trees, fruits and plants, there is a great difference from those of Juana. In this island, there are many spices and great mines of gold and of other metals.

The people of this island and of all the other islands which I have found and of which I have information, all go naked, men and women, as their mothers bore them, although some of the women cover a single place with the leaf of a plant or with a net of cotton which they make for the purpose. They have no iron or steel or weapons, nor are they fitted to use them. This is not because they are not well built and of handsome stature, but because they are very marvellously timorous. They have no other arms than spears made of canes, cut in seeding time, to the ends of which they fix a small sharpened stick. Of these they do not dare to make use, for many times it has happened that I have sent ashore two or three men to some town to have speech with them, and countless people have come out to them, and as soon as they have seen my men approaching, they have fled, a father not even waiting for his son. This is not because ill has been done to any one of them; on the contrary, at every place where I have been and have been able to have speech with them, I have given to them of that which I had, such as cloth and many other things, receiving nothing in exchange. But so they are, incurably timid. It is true that, after they have been reassured and have lost this fear, they are so guileless and so generous with all that they possess, that no one would believe it who has not seen it. They refuse nothing that they possess, if it be asked of them; on the contrary, they invite any one to share it and display as much love as if they would give their hearts. They are content with whatever trifle of whatever kind that may be given to them, whether it be of value or valueless. I forbade that they should be given

Eñor por que se que aureis plazer dela grand
victoria que nro señor me ha dado en mi vyaie
vos escriuo esta por la ql sabreys como é xxxiij
dias pase alas jndias cola armada que los illu
striffimos Rey z reyna nros señores me dieron
donde yo falle muy muchas Islas pobladas con gête syn
numero. y dellas todas he tomado poseffió por sus altezas
con pregon y vâdera real estêdida y nõ me fue côtradicho.
Ala primera q yo falle puse nôbre sant saluador a comemo
racion de su alta mageftad el qual marauillosa mête todo
efto andado los jndios la llamâ guanabam. Ala segûda pu
se nôbre la ysa de stã maria de côcepcion, ala tercera ferrâdi
na, ala quarta la ysabella. Ala quinta la isla Juana, z asy a
cada vna nôbre nueuo Quâdo yo llegue ala juana segui yo
la cofta della al ponête y la falle tan grâde q pensé q seria
tierra firma, la puincia decatayo y como no falle asi villas
y lugares enla cofta dela mar saluo pequeñas poblaciones
con la gête delas qles non podia hauer fabla por q luego
fuyâ todos andaua yo adelâte por el dicho camino penfan
do de no errar grâdes Ciudades o villas y al cabo d mu
chas leguas vifto q no hauia inopacion y q la cofta me le
uaua al fetêtrion de adôde mi voluad era contraria por q
el puierno era ya encarnado yo tenia ppofito de hazer dl al
auftro y tanbiê el viêto me dio adelante determine de no a
guardar otro tiêpo y bolui atras fafta vn señalado puerto
d adôde enbie dos hôbres por la tierra pa saber fi auia rey
o grâdes ciudades andouierô tres iornadas y hallarô infi
nitas poblaciôes pequeñas y gête fin numero mas no co
fa de regimiêto por lo qual fe boluierô yo entêdia barta de
otros jndios q ya tenia tomados como côtinua mête efta
tierra era ifla z afi segui la cofta della al ouête ciêto y fiete
leguas fafta dôde fazia fin; del qual cabo vi otra ifla al ouê

First page of the Spanish edition of the Columbus letter, 1497.

things so worthless as fragments of broken crockery, scraps of broken glass and lace tips, although when they were able to get them, they fancied that they possessed the best jewel in the world. So it was found that for a thong a sailor received gold to the weight of two and a half castellanos, and others received much more for other things which were worth less. As for new blancas, for them they would give everything which they had, although it might be two or three castellanos' weight of gold or an arroba or two of spun cotton. They took even the pieces of the broken hoops of the wine barrels and, like savages, gave what they had, so that it seemed to me to be wrong and I forbade it. I gave them a thousand handsome good things, which I had brought, in order that they might conceive affection for us and, more than that, might become Christians and be inclined to the love and service of Your Highnesses and of the whole Castilian nation, and strive to collect and give us of the things which they have in abundance and which are necessary to us.

They do not hold any creed nor are they idolaters; but they all believe that power and good are in the heavens and were very firmly convinced that I, with these ships and men, came from the heavens, and in this belief they everywhere received me after they had mastered their fear. This belief is not the result of ignorance, for they are, on the contrary, of a very acute intelligence and they are men who navigate all those seas, so that it is amazing how good an account they give of everything. It is because they have never seen people clothed or ships of such a kind.

As soon as I arrived in the Indies, in the first island which I found, I took some of the natives by force, in order that they might learn and might give me information of whatever there is in these parts. And so it was that they soon understood us, and we them, either by speech or signs, and they have been very serviceable. At present, those I bring with me are still of the opinion that I come from Heaven, for all the intercourse which they have had with me. They were the first to announce this wherever I went, and the others went running from house to house, and to the neighbouring towns, with loud cries of, "Come! Come! See the men from Heaven!" So all came, men and women alike, when their minds were set at rest concerning us, not one,

The Grand Khan; in John Mandeville's *Libro de las meravillas del mundo*, 1524.

small or great, remaining behind, and they all brought something to eat and drink, which they gave with extraordinary affection.

In all the islands, they have very many canoes, which are like rowing fustas, some larger and some smaller; some are greater than a fusta of eighteen benches. They are not so broad, because they are made of a single log of wood, but a fusta would not keep up with them in rowing, since their speed is an incredible thing. In these they navigate among all those islands, which are innumerable, and carry their goods. I have seen one of these canoes with seventy or eighty men in it, each one with his paddle.

In all these islands, I saw no great diversity in the appearance of the people or in their manners and language. On the contrary, they all understand one another, which is a very curious thing, on account of which I hope that their Highnesses will determine upon their conversion to our holy faith, towards which they are very inclined.

I have already said how I went one hundred and seven leagues in a straight line from west to east along the seashore of the island of Juana, and as a result of this voyage I can say that this island is larger than England and Scotland together, for, beyond these one hundred and seven leagues, there remain to the westward two provinces to which I have not gone. One of these provinces they call "Avan," [2] and there people are born with tails. These provinces cannot have a length of less than fifty or sixty leagues, as I could understand from those Indians whom I have and who know all the islands.

The other island, Española, has a circumference greater than all Spain from Collioure by the seacoast to Fuenterabia in Vizcaya, for I voyaged along one side for one hundred and eighty-eight great leagues in a straight line from west to east. It is a land to be desired and, when seen, never to be left. I have taken possession of all for their Highnesses, and all are more richly endowed than I know how or am able to say, and I hold all for their Highnesses, so that they may dispose of them as they do of the kingdoms of Castile and as absolutely. But especially, in this Española, in the situation most convenient and in the best position for the mines of gold and for all trade as well with the mainland here as with that there, belonging to the Grand Khan, where will be great trade and profit, I have taken possession of a large town, to which I gave the name "Villa de Navidad," and in it I have made fortifications and a fort, which will now by this time be entirely completed. In it I have left enough men for such a purpose with arms and artillery and provisions for more than a year, and a fusta, and one, a master of all seacraft, to build others, and I have established great friendship with the king of that land, so much so, that he was proud to call me "brother" and to treat me as such. And even were he to change his attitude to one of hostility towards these men, he and his do not know what arms are. They go naked, as I have already said, and they are the most timorous people in the world, so that the men whom I have left there alone would suffice to destroy all that land, and the island is without danger for their persons, if they know how to govern themselves. [3]

In all these islands, it seems to me that all men are content with one woman, and to their chief or king they give as many as twenty.

Human monstrosities; in John Mandeville's *Libro de las meravillas del mundo*, 1524.

It appears to me that the women work more than do the men. I have not been able to learn if they hold private property; it seemed to me to be that all took a share in whatever any one had, especially of eatable things.

In these islands I have so far found no human monstrosities, [4] as many expected, but on the contrary the whole population is very well formed, nor are they negroes as in Guinea, but their hair is flowing and they are not born where there is intense force in the rays of the sun. It is true that the sun there has great power, although it is distant from the equinoctial line twenty-six degrees. [5] In these islands, where there are high mountains, the cold was severe this winter, but they endure it, being used to it and with the help of meats which they consume with many and extremely hot spices. Thus I have found no monsters, nor had a report of any, except in an island "Carib," which is the second at the coming into the Indies, and which is inhabited by a people who are regarded in all the islands as very fierce and who eat human flesh. They have many canoes with which they range through all the islands of India and pillage and take whatever they can. They are no more malformed than are the others, except that they have the custom of wearing their hair long like women, and they use bows and arrows of the same cane stems, with a small piece of wood at the end, owing to their lack of iron which they do not possess. They are ferocious among these other people who are cowardly to an excessive degree, but I make no more account of them than of the rest. These are they who have intercourse with the women of "Matinino," which is the first island met on the way from Spain to the Indies, in which there is not a man. These women engage in no feminine occupation, but use bows and arrows of cane, like those already mentioned, and they arm and protect themselves with plates of copper, of which they have much.

In another island, which they assure me is larger than Española, the people have no hair. In it there is incalculable gold, and from it and from the other islands I bring with me Indians as evidence.

In conclusion, to speak only of what has been accomplished on this voyage, which was so hasty, their Highnesses can see that I will give them as much gold as they may need, if their Highnesses will render me very slight assistance; presently, I will give them spices and cotton, as much as their Highnesses shall command; and mastic, as much as they shall order to be shipped and which, up to now, has been found only in Greece, in the island of Chios, and the Seignory sells it for what it pleases [6]; and aloe, as much as they shall order to be shipped; and slaves, as many as they shall order, and who will be from the idolaters. I believe also that I have found rhubarb and cinnamon, and I shall find a thousand other things of value, which the people whom I have left there will have discovered, for I have not delayed at any point, so far as the wind allowed me to sail, except in the town of Navidad, in order to leave it secured and well established, and in truth I should have done much more if the ships had served me as reason demanded.

This is enough. And thus the eternal God, Our Lord, gives to all those who walk in His way triumph over things which appear to be impossible, and this was notably one. For, although men have talked or have written of these lands, all was conjectural, without ocular evidence, but amounted only to this, that those who heard for the most part listened and judged rather by hearsay than from even a small something tangible. So that, since Our Redeemer has given the victory to our most illustrious King and Queen, and to their renowned kingdoms, in so great a matter, for this all Christendom ought to feel delight and make great feasts and give solemn thanks to the Holy Trinity, with many solemn prayers for the great exaltation which they shall have in the turning of so many peoples to our holy faith, and afterwards for the temporal benefits, because not only Spain but all Christendom will have hence refreshment and gain.

This is an account of the facts, thus abridged.

Done in the caravel, off the Canary Islands, [7] on the fifteenth day of February, in the year one thousand four hundred and ninety-three.

At your orders.

THE ADMIRAL.

After having written this, and being in the sea of Castile, there came upon me so great a south and south-east wind [8] that I was obliged to ease the ship. But I ran here to-day into this port of Lisbon, which was the greatest marvel in the world, whence I decided to write to their Highnesses. In all the Indies, I have always found weather like May. There I went in thirty-three days and I should have returned in twenty-eight, save for these storms which have detained me for fourteen days, beating about in this sea. Here all the sailors say that never has there been so bad a winter nor so many ships lost.

Done on the fourth day of March.

Notes to the Journal

1 The expulsion of the Jews was ordered on March 31, 1492. On April 17th, Ferdinand and Isabel signed the letters patent authorizing Columbus to undertake his voyage.

2 The Saltés bar is at the entrance of the bay formed by the junction of two rivers: Rio Tinto and Odiel. The town of Palos is on the Rio Tinto, three miles upstream. About two-thirds of the men who accompanied Columbus on his first voyage were from the Tinto - Odiel area.

3 Columbus probably used the Roman or Italian mile of 1480 meters, or 4850 feet, which is roughly three-fourths of the nautical mile (6080 feet). Readers who wish to convert the distances indicated in the *Journal* into nautical miles should keep in mind that Columbus' sea league of four Roman miles was equivalent to about three nautical miles.

4 Martin Alonso Pinzón was captain of the *Pinta*. His brother, Francisco, served under him as master. A third brother, Vicente Yañez, captained the *Niña*. The Pinzóns were from Palos.

5 Cristóbal Quintero, owner of the *Pinta*, and Gomez Rascón were both from Palos and made the voyage as able seamen. Quintero also took part in Columbus' third voyage as owner and master of a caravel named *Santa Maria de Guia*.

6 This volcano is the Pico de Teide (12,200 feet).

7 Doña Inés de Peraza was not Guillem's mother, but his grandmother. She had inherited from her father, Hernan de Peraza, the islands of Hierro and Gomera, which

had been made into a county for herself and her descendants. She was still alive in 1493. Her son having been killed in a native uprising in 1487, her grandson, Guillem, inherited from her the title of Count of Gomera. Her daughter-in-law, Isabel de Bobadilla, was Guillem's mother, and Columbus is reported to have fallen in love with her.

8   Because of peculiar atmospheric conditions, a phantom island is seen from time to time in the twilight west of the Canaries. A photograph of it appeared recently in the Madrid newspaper *ABC* (August 10, 1958).

9   In 1484 a resident of Madeira, Fernan Domingues do Arco, was granted by King John II of Portugal the governorship of an island which he hoped to discover. Columbus was probably living in Madeira at the time.

10   On this day Columbus noticed the diurnal rotation of the North Star (Polaris), noted also on September 17th and 30th. See S. E. Morison, "Columbus and Polaris," *The American Neptune*, vol. 1, 1940, pp. 1-20.

11   To Columbus, the high sea of September 23rd, which calmed his men and made them more willing to follow him, was a miracle, a manifestation of God, which he compares to the miracle of the Red Sea.

12   These islands were probably the legendary islands of St. Brendan, Brazil, Antilla and the Seven Cities which were pictured on fifteenth century maps.

13   *Dorado* is the name usually given in Spanish and in English to the *coriphaena*, a fish of the tropics, about four feet long, with a vivid, almost metallic colouring, which feeds on flying fish and follows ships.

14   The guards are β and Υ, the two stars of the Little Dipper (Ursa Minor) furthest from the North Star. As they swing around the pole, their position in relation to Polaris was used to tell the time at night. For that purpose "a figure of a little man was drawn with feet together, outstretched arms and Polaris on his breast" (S. E. Morison, "Columbus and Polaris," p. 3).

15   *Cipangu* was the name given to Japan.

16   The manuscript has "west-southeast," which does not make sense. The correction was first made by Fernández de Navarrete. Errors in rhumbs are frequent in the manuscript.

17   Rodrigo de Triana. There was no one by such name in the ships' lists. Rodrigo's real name probably was Juan Rodriguez Bermeo.

18   The *veedor*, or comptroller, was an appointee of the Sovereigns. He was to keep a record of all the gold, precious stones and spices, and to make sure that the Crown would not be cheated out of its share.

19   It is generally taken for granted that Guanahani was Watlings Island. Recently, however, there have been some dissenters (P. Verhoog, Edwin A. and Marion C. Links) who think that Columbus first landed on the Caicos. In the latest study on the subject, E. Roukema rejects their views and restates the case for Watlings Island (*American*

Neptune, vol. XIX, April, 1959). We refer the readers who might be interested in this controversy to the bibliography.

20   Rodrigo de Escobedo, *escribano mayor* (chief clerk or recorder), and Pedro Gutier-rez were among those who remained on Española. They were later killed by the Indians.

21   The *ceotis* (correct form: *ceitil*) was a copper coin first minted to commemorate the capture of Ceuta by the Portuguese in 1415. The *blanca* was a copper coin worth half a *maravedi.* There were 750 *blancas* in a gold ducat. The *arroba* was a measure of weight equivalent to 25 pounds or a fourth of a quintal.

22   *Santa Maria de Concepción.* Rum Cay. In my identifications of place names given in the *Journal* I usually follow S. E. Morison.

23   The Spanish text is incoherent because of a lacuna in the manuscript.

24   The *maravedi* was a copper coin worth two *blancas.* There were 375 *maravedis* in a gold ducat.

25   *Fernandina.* Long Island.

26   The plural used here probably refers to both Rum Cay and Conception Island, which are very close to each other.

27   The Spanish word is *agujeta.* It means a thong or a leather string with metal tips, used for lacing boots, breeches, doublets and other wearing apparel.

28   Terce. Nine o'clock in the morning.

29   Las Casas' marginal note: "These chimneys do not serve to let out the smoke, but are cornices which they have on their thatch roofs. To let out the smoke, they just leave an opening in the roof."

30   *Castellano.* A gold coin. In 1480 its value was set at 480 *maravedis.*

31   *Isabella.* Crooked Island.

32   *Cabo Hermoso.* Southern tip of Fortune Island.

33   *Cabo de la Laguna.* Southwest point of Crooked Island, facing the northern tip of Fortune Island, from which it is separated by a very narrow inlet.

34   *Cabo del Isleo.* Northwestern point of Crooked Island.

35   The *palmo* was a measure of length, equivalent to eight inches.

36   *Colba* is Cuba, and *Bohio* is Santo Domingo.

37   *Quisay,* or *Quinsay,* was the name given by Marco Polo to the capital of the Grand Khan.

38   *Islas de Arena.* The Ragged Islands.

39 *San Salvador* (Cuba). Bahia Bariay.

40 *Rio de la Luna*. Rio Jururu.

41 *Rio de Mares*. Puerto Gibara.

42 "Skulls." Las Casas' marginal note: "They must be skulls of seacows."

43 *La Pena de los Enamorados* (Lovers' Leap) is a rock half way between Antequera and Archidona, in Andalusia. According to a fifteenth century legend, a Christian warrior and his Moorish beloved leaped to their death from the rock to escape their pursuers.

44 *Cabo de los Palmas*. Punta Uvero.

45 Luis de Torres, a converted Jew, was the interpreter of the expedition. He was among those left behind in Española, where he was killed by the Indians. Rodrigo de Jeres may have been the sailor who had lived in Guinea and whom Columbus thought of sending to the Grand Khan on October 30th.

46 The correct latitude is 20°. Morison thinks that Columbus may have mistaken Alfirk (B of the constellation *Cepheus*) for Polaris.

47 *Bohio*. Marginal note of Las Casas: "The Indians of those islands called their houses *bohio*. The admiral did not understand it well." Columbus thought that *bohio* was the name of an island, and he applied it to Haiti. Today *bohio* means 'hut' in Cuba.

48 In a marginal note, Las Casas identifies the *mames* or *ajes* with the sweet potato (*boniata*).

49 Master Diego probably was a physician or an apothecary.

50 These herbs must have been dried tobacco leaves. Columbus mentions them for the first time on October 15th.

51 *Babeque* (also spelt *Baveque* or *Baneque*) probably was Great Inagua Island.

52 *Rio del Sol*. Punta Sama.

53 According to Morison, Columbus mistook the gumbo-limbo for the mastic, and the agave for the aloe. Most of Columbus' identifications of trees and plants are only approximate.

54 *Cabo Cuba*. Punta Lucrezia. See the map of Juan de la Cosa, drawn in 1500.

55 This may have been the entrance to Nipé Bay.

56 *Mar de Nuestra Señora*. Tanamo Bay.

57 *Taso* or *Taxo*. Taxel or badger. There are no badgers in Cuba.

58 Probably a trunkfish.

59 Las Casas' marginal note: "They must have been *hutias*." *Hutias* are small quadru-

peds, about the size of a rabbit, which dwell in trees and live on fruit and insects. They are comestible.

60   The reference to Florida was added to the text of the *Journal* by Las Casas. Florida was not discovered until 1513.

61   There is some confusion. Although the *Sea of Nuestra Señora* (Tanamo Bay) is mentioned, the harbour described here is Puerto Cayo Moa, and the flat island is Cayo Moa Grande. Yet Las Casas insists that Columbus returned to the *Sea of Nuestra Señora* on Saturday, November 24th. (See entry in the *Journal* on Wednesday, November 14th: "He did not enter it more than to see it from without, until another visit, which he made on the Saturday of the following week, as will appear here.") This contradiction is very puzzling.

62   *Cabo el Pico.* Punta Guarico. See La Cosa's map.

63   *Cabo Campana.* Punta Plata or Punta Baez.

64   This mountain is El Yunque, "the evil-shaped mountain that can be seen fifty miles away, a landmark known to everyone who navigates these waters" (S. E. Morison).

65   Baracoa Harbour. Columbus called it *Puerto Santo*. See La Cosa's map.

66   A *fusta* is a small galley.

67   *Cabo Lindo.* Punta del Fraile. See La Cosa's map.

68   The Windward Passage, between Cuba and Haiti.

69   *Cabo Maisi.* See La Cosa's map.

70   *Puerto Maria.* Port St. Nicolas (Haiti). A few hours later Columbus changed the name to St. Nicolas, because it was that saint's day. *Puerto de S. Nicolas* appears on La Cosa's map.

71   *Cabo Estrella.* Cape St. Nicolas. See La Cosa's map.

72   *Cabo Elefante.* One of the points at the foot of Haut-Piton, either Grande Pointe of Pointe Palmiette. *Cabo Cinquin* is Pointe Jean Rabel.

73   *Tortuga.* The Ile de la Tortue, where French buccaneers founded an independent republic in the seventeenth century.

74   The manuscript has "thirty-four miles." We have substituted "three to four miles," which is the correction suggested by Navarrete and by Morison.

75   Morison suggests reading "miles" for "leagues."

76   *Puerto de la Concepción.* Moustique Bay.

77   The birds Columbus mistook for nightingales were probably mocking birds.

78   *Niame* (in modern Spanish, *ñame*; in English, yam). A tubercule used for food.

79   The correct latitude is 20°.

80   *Valle del Paraiso*. Throughout the Spanish regime, this valley was known as Valparaiso. The *Rio Guadalquivir* is Trois-Rivières.

81   This village probably stood on the site of Port-de-Paix.

82   The commemoration of the Annunciation (December 18th) is popularly called *Santa Maria de la O*, because most of the hymns sung on that day begin with the letter 'O'.

83   The *excelente* was a gold coin whose value had been set at two castellanos, or 960 maravedis, in 1480. It contained about nine grams of gold.

84   *Dos Hermanos*. Probably two hillocks west of Acul Bay.

85   *Cabo Torres*. Cap au Borgne. See La Cosa's map.

86   *Santo Tomas*. Marigot? Limbé Islet?

87   *Cabo Alto y Bajo*. Pointe Limbé.

88   *Monte Caribata*. Mont Haut du Cap.

89   The Baie d'Acul. This bay was named after a lady who resided there and was very hospitable to sailors. The original Spanish name was *Acon de Luysa*.

90   Columbus was in England in 1477.

91   The chufa, vulgarly called *juncia avellanada*, is a small tubercule, produced by a reed-like plant, the *juncia*. From it is extracted a refreshing drink, very popular in Spain, known as *horchata* (orgeade), whitish in colour and nutty in taste. Some varieties of it grow in Cuba and Santo Domingo. Apparently the Indians ate the small tubercules as we do nuts.

92   *La Amiga*. Ile des Rats.

93   The Baie des Francais.

94   *Punta Santa*. Pointe Nicolet or Pointe St. Honoré. Both points are near Cape Haïtien.

95   One of the reefs facing the beach of Limonade-Bord-de-Mer. See map in S. E. Morison, "The Route of Columbus along the North Coast of Haiti and the Site of Navidad," in *Transactions of the American Philosophical Society*, vol. xxxi, December, 1940.

96   A cousin of Beatriz de Arana, Columbus' mistress, Diego de Arana was *alguacil*, or marshal of the fleet. Columbus left him in command of the fort at Navidad, where Diego and all his men were later killed by the Indians.

97   The village was probably near the present site of Caracol, where there is an Indian mound. Its chief, or *cacique*, Guacanagari, remained a friend of Columbus even after the massacre of the Spanish garrison at Navidad.

98   *Caçabi* or *cazaba*. Bread made from the root of the yucca.

99   I translate the word *cava* by 'moat' and not by 'cellar' — as most translators have done before me — because *cava* usually meant 'ditch' or 'moat' in medieval and Renaissance Spanish; and also because a cellar in the rainy West Indian climate would be absolutely useless, particularly if — as Morison asserts — the fort was built on Limonade Beach, where a cellar would quickly fill with water. Spanish garrisons in the West Indies and Florida usually kept their supplies in warehouses above ground.

100   The *despensero mayor* was the chief butler of the King's table. He generally belonged to the upper nobility.

101   *Cabo de la Sierpe*. Pointe Jacquezi?

102   *Monte Christi*. This name has survived. The sandy islets to the west are known today as the Seven Brothers (Siete Hermanos). See La Cosa's map.

103   *Cabo Bezerro*. Punta Chica?

104   *Yamaye*. Jamaica.

105   *Rio de Oro*. Yaque del Norte.

106   *Punta Roja*. Punta Rucia.

107   The sirens were probably seacows.

108   The Malagueta Coast (Liberia, Sierra Leone) was named after a variety of pepper, the *malagueta*, which grows there.

109   *Rio de Gracia*. Today, Puerto de Gracia.

110   *Cabo Bel Prado*. Such a cape appears on the La Cosa map which was drawn in 1500. The modern name is Punta Patilla.

111   *Monte de Plata*. The seaport of Puerto Plata got its name from this mountain. On La Cosa's map, *Cabo de Plata*.

112   *Cabo del Angél*. Punta Payne (or Punta Sosua). The gulf between it and Puerto Plata is called the Bahia de Santiago.

113   *Cabo del Hierro*. Today, Punta Macoris.

114   *Punta Seca*. Punta Cabarete.

115   *Cabo Redondo*. Cabo de la Roca.

116   *Cabo Francés* still bears the same name today; but the name originally given to it by Columbus must have been *Cabo Franco*, for such a cape is figured on the La Cosa map. The bay mentioned to the west of it in the *Journal* is the Baya Escocesa.

117   *Cabo del Buen Tiempo*. Punta del Aguila?

118   *Cabo Tajado*. The name has survived, but this cape is also called Punta Sabaneta.

119 *Cabo Padre e Hijo*. Cape Cabrón.

120 *Cabo del Enamorado*. Cape Samana.

121 The bay is Samana Bay, and the islet near which Columbus anchored is called Cayo Levantado.

122 *Matinino*. Martinique, one of the French Antilles.

123 According to Las Casas, it was a heavy round stick, a sort of bludgeon, made of palm wood and hard enough to crack a man's skull even if he was wearing a helmet.

124 *Golfo de las Flechas*. This is the name which Columbus gave to Samana Bay after the encounter with the natives. On its northern shore, there is a village still called Punta de las Flechas.

125 *San Teramo*. Las Casas identifies it in a marginal note with Cape Engano, the easternmost point of Santo Domingo.

126 Conil belonged to the Duke of Medina Sidonia, while Cadiz was the fief of the Ponce de Leon family until January, 1493, when it was annexed to the Crown. In 1494 and 1495 the income derived from the Cadiz fisheries was used by Queen Isabel to finance the expedition to Santo Domingo.

127 The *rabiforcado* is not a fish, but a bird (a frigate-bird). It may be that Las Casas read '*pescado*' for '*pajaro*'. In several instances Las Casas reports that he is having difficulty in reading the text of the *Journal* because of the bad lettering of the manuscript.

128 There are two errors in the entry for January 22nd: first, eight half hour glasses at eight miles an hour make thirty-two miles, not seventy-two; second, eleven half hour glasses at six leagues an hour do not make seven leagues. (See J. W. McElroy, "The Ocean Navigation of Columbus on his First Voyage," *American Neptune*, 1941, p. 232.

129 Vicente Yañez, brother of Martin Alonso Pinzón, was captain of the *Niña*. He made several voyages to America and died in 1514.

130 Bartolomé Roldan was booked as able seaman, but served as assistant pilot.

131 Pero Alonso Niño, brother of Juan Niño who owned the *Niña*, had been pilot of the wrecked *Santa Maria*. He made several voyages to America, including one to the coast of Venezuela (1499-1500).

132 Sancho Ruiz de Gama was pilot of the *Niña*.

133 *Nafé*, or *Anaffé*, is today Casablanca (Morocco). It was captured and dismantled by the Portuguese in 1468.

134 *Guadalupe*. A famous shrine in Spanish Estremadura.

135 "Orphaned of father and mother." This would be true in the case of Diego, Columbus' legitimate son, whose mother appears to have died in Portugal before 1485; but Beatriz de Arana, mother of his bastard son Fernando, was alive and residing in Cordoba.

136 Juan de Castañeda (correct name: João da Castanheira) was only acting governor in the absence of the captain, João Soares, who had gone to Lisbon to be married.

137 "Complines." In Catholic ritual, the last prayer of the day, recited after nightfall.

138 *Cascaes.* It was then a fishing village at the mouth of the Tagus. Today it is a fashionable summer resort.

139 *Rastelo.* Today, a suburb of Lisbon, four miles downstream. In 1493 it was Lisbon's outport.

140 This Bartolomé Diaz has been identified by many historians as the Bartolomé Dias who discovered the Cape of Good Hope in 1486. There is no proof for this identification. Bartolomé Diaz (or Dias) was then a very common name in both Portugal and Spain.

141 *Noroña.* This distinguished family descended from a bastard son of King Henry II of Castile, who had married the daughter of King Ferdinand I of Portugal.

142 *Sacaven.* A small town north of Lisbon, famous today for its pottery.

143 *Valparaiso.* King John II of Portugal resided at the time in the Franciscan monastery of Santa Maria das Virtudes, in a fertile valley called Valle do Paraiso, some thirty miles north of Lisbon.

144 *La Mina* was a Portuguese colony in West Africa.

145 *Crato.* A priory belonging to the order of St. John of Jerusalem (Knights of the Hospital). It was very wealthy and included in its territory twelve towns and twenty-nine parishes. Its prior was usually a prince of royal blood or a member of the upper aristocracy.

146 The monastery of San Antonio da Castanheira is on the Tagus, north of Lisbon.

147 The duke was evidently the Queen's brother, Dom Manuel, Duke of Beja, and heir to the throne. He succeeded John II in 1495. As for the marquis, Morison thinks that he may have been Martin de Noroña's father.

148 *Alhandra.* A small town north of Lisbon.

149 The *espadim* was a gold coin minted only during the reign of John II.

150 *Faro.* A seaport, capital of Algarve, southernmost province of Portugal. Many Portuguese sea-faring men and many settlers of Madeira and the Azores came from Algarve.

151 A few hours later and on the same tide arrived the *Pinta*, commanded by Martin Alonso Pinzón. She had escaped the storm off the Azores and had made port at Bayona (Galicia) toward the end of February. From there she set sail for Palos, crossing the Saltés bar on March 15th. Martin Alonso died about three weeks later, possibly of syphilis contracted in the Indies.

152 "Save for some servants of God." This is an allusion of Las Casas to himself and his fellow Dominicans who took up the struggle for justice to the Indians against the greed and cruelty of the early Spanish settlers.

Notes to the letter

1 In the Latin version of the letter, printed in Rome in May, 1493, these distances are rendered in miles instead of leagues, at the rate of three miles to a league. It seems that Columbus used two kinds of leagues: a sea league of four Roman miles, and a land league of three Roman miles or less.

2 *Avan* was the name for the northern part of Cuba. From it is derived the name Havana.

3 Unfortunately, they did not. They quarrelled and fought among themselves, split into small groups, became odious to the Indians and were all killed.

4 These monsters were reported to exist in India and China and were described in the *Travels of John Mandeville*, a fourteenth century work which enjoyed wide popularity. Its author related a lot of tall tales about countries which he had never visited.

5 The correct latitude is 20° to 21°.

6 The island of Chios was a Genoese possession until 1560. It was governed by a commercial corporation called the *Maona*, which held a monopoly on the mastic trade. Columbus appears to have been in Chios in 1474 or 1475.

7 "Off the Canary Islands." Evidently a misprint. On February 15th, Columbus was off the Azores, not the Canaries.

8 Morison suggests reading "southwest" instead of "southeast."

Bibliography

BALLESTEROS BERETTA, ANTONIO. *Cristóbal Colón y el descubrimento de América*, 2 vols. Barcelona, 1945.

CADDEO, RINALDO. *Giornale di bordo di Cristoforo Colombo*, Milano, 1939.

CARBIA, ROMULO D. "La supercheria en la historia del descubrimento de América, *Humanidades* (La Plata), vol. XX (1930), pp. 169-185.

CASAS, BARTOLOMÉ DE LAS. *Historia de Indias*, edited by A. Millares Carlo, Mexico, 1951.

CASAS, BARTOLOMÉ DE LAS. *Historia de Indias*, edited by Pérez de Tudela, 2 vols. Madrid, 1957.

COLOMBO, FERNANDO. *Historie del S. D. Fernando Colombo*, Venice, 1571.

FERNÁNDEZ DE NAVARRETE, MARTIN. *Viajes de Cristóbal Colón*, Madrid, 1941. (Reprinting of the first volume of the *Colección de Viajes*, 1825.)

GOULD, ALICE B. "Nueva lista documentada de los tripulantes de Colón en 1492," *Boletin de la Real Academia de la Historia* (Madrid), vols. 85-88, 90, 92, 110, 111.

GOULD, R. T. "The Landfall of Columbus: An Old Problem Restated," *The Geographical Journal*, vol. LXIX (1927), pp. 403-429.

GUILLÉN TATO, JULIO F. *El primer viaje de Cristóbal Colón*, Madrid, 1943.

GUILLÉN TATO, JULIO F. *La parla marinera en el diario del primer viaje de Cristóbal Colón*, Madrid, 1951.

GUILLÉN TATO, JULIO F. *La caravela Santa Maria*, Madrid, 1927.

HANKE, LEWIS AND JIMÉNEZ FERNÁNDEZ, MANUEL. *Bartolomé de las Casas, Bibliografia critica*, Santiago de Chile, 1954.

HARRISSE, HENRY. *Christophe Colomb*, Paris, 1884.

JANE, CECIL. *The Voyages of Christopher Columbus*, London, 1930.

JOS, EMILIANO. "El libro del primer viaje. Algunas ediciones recientes," *Miscellanea Americanista* (Madrid), vol. II (1951), pp. 121-153.

LINK, EDWIN A. AND MARION C. "A New Theory on Columbus' Voyage through the Bahamas," *Smithsonian Miscellaneous Collections* (Washington), vol. CXXXV, no. 4 (1958), pp. 1-32.

MCELROY, JOHN W. "The Ocean Navigation of Columbus on his First Voyage," *The American Neptune*, vol. 1 (1941), pp. 209-240.

MENÉNDEZ PIDAL, RAMON. *La lengua de Cristóbal Colón*, Madrid, 1942.

MERRIEN, JEAN. *Christophe Colomb*, Paris, 1955.

MORISON, SAMUEL ELIOT. *Christopher Columbus, Admiral of the Ocean Sea*, 2 vols., Boston, 1942.

MORISON, SAMUEL ELIOT. *Christopher Columbus, Mariner*, London, 1957.

MORISON, SAMUEL ELIOT. "Columbus and Polaris," *The American Neptune*, vol. 1, no. 1 (1940), pp. 1-35.

MORISON, SAMUEL ELIOT. "Texts and Translations of the Journal of Columbus' First Voyage," *Hispanic American Historical Review*, vol. XIX (August, 1939), pp. 235-261.

MUGRIDGE, DONALD. *Christopher Columbus, A Selected List of Books and Articles Published by American Authors or Published in America, 1892-1950*, Washington, 1950.

MURO OREJÓN, ANTONIO. *Cristóbal Colón. El original de la capitulación de 1942 y sus copias contemporaneas*, Seville, 1951.

Raccolta di documenti e studi pubblicati dalla R. Commissione Colombiana per il quarto centenario della scoperta dell'America, 13 vols., Rome, 1892-96.

ROUKEMA, E. "Columbus Landed on Watlings Island," *The American Neptune*, vol. XIX, no. 2 (April, 1959), pp. 79-113.

RUMEU DE ARMAS, ANTONIO. *Colón en Barcelona*, Seville, 1944.

SÁ NOGUEIRA, RODRIGO DE. "Portuguesismos en Cristovão Colombo," *Miscelanea de Filologia, Literatura e Historia Cultural a Memoria de Francisco Adolfo Coelho*, Lisbon, 1950, pp. 81-107.

SANZ, CARLOS. *Bibliografía general de la carta de Colón*, Madrid, 1958.

SANZ, CARLOS. *La carta de Colón anunciando la llegada a las Indias*, Madrid, 1958. Facsimile reproductions of the seventeen known editions.

TAYLOR, E. G. R. "The Navigating Manual of Columbus," *Journal of the Institute of Navigation*, vol. V, no. 1 (January, 1952).

TORRE Y DEL CERRO, JOSÉ DE LA. *Beatriz Enriquez de Harana y Cristóbal Colón*, Madrid, 1933.

VERHOOG, PIETER. "Columbus Landed on Caicos," *Proceedings of the United States Naval Institute*, vol. LXXX, no. 10 (1955), pp. 1101-1110.

VERHOOG, PIETER. *Guanahani Again*, Amsterdam, 1947.

VIGNAUD, HENRY. *Histoire de la grande entreprise de Christophe Colomb*, 2 vols., Paris, 1911.

The Cartography of Columbus' First Voyage

Maps in the formation of Columbus' ideas.

According to Ferdinand Columbus, his father's speculation on the possibility of discovering the Indies by a westerly voyage sprang from the Portuguese navigation to Guinea. "It was in Portugal that the Admiral began to think that, if men could sail so far south, one might also sail west and find land in that quarter."

Columbus' eager search for authorities to support his hypothesis is exemplified in his annotations (*postille*) to the works of classical and mediaeval cosmographers, notably Seneca and Pierre d'Ailly. Both in the *postille* and in Ferdinand's *Historie* we find the basic concept underlying Columbus' plan for the enterprise of the Indies, namely his estimate of the width of the ocean between Europe and Asia, expressed in degrees and converted, by a calculation peculiar to himself, into miles and sailing time. From his reading, supplemented by the correspondence with Toscanelli between 1474 and 1481, Columbus arrived at the conclusion that Cipangu lay about 80 degrees west of the Canaries, and the coast of Cathay some 30 degrees further west.

His interpretation of the Moslem geographer Alfragan, controlled by observations made on Portuguese voyages to Africa in 1485-8, led Columbus to evaluate the equatorial degree as 56 2/3 Roman miles or 45 nautical miles, — "the shortest estimate of the degree ever made," in Professor Morison's words.

But Columbus was a cartographer, and it cannot be doubted that he also sought graphic expression for his theoretical concepts in globes and maps, to which indeed the *Journal* refers (e. g. on October 24th and November 14th, 1492). The characteristics of the cartographic sources consulted by Columbus can be readily determined. They must have reflected the views of Toscanelli (derived from Marinus of Tyre and from Marco Polo) on the longitudinal extension of Asia, and on the width of the ocean; and they must have provided a precise quantitative statement of these distances, in terms of degrees.

The world map or chart which Toscanelli sent to Lisbon in 1474, and later to Columbus, has not survived, but it is possible to reconstruct it from the data given in his letter; the most convincing reconstruction is that of Hermann Wagner. From this map Columbus obtained a figure of 26 'spaces,' that is 130 degrees, for the width of the ocean (which presumably occupied the centre of the map) between Lisbon and Quinsay, on the coast of Cathay. Toscanelli also laid down, in the ocean, the island of Antillia, which is found in many nautical charts of the 15th century; and, 10 spaces (50 degrees) further west, Cipangu.

We cannot as yet point to any extant cartographic work executed before 1492, and embodying Toscanelli's concepts, that could have come to Columbus' notice. The globes to which he alludes in his *Journal* have disappeared; and no non-Ptolemaic map of the 15th century graduated in longitude has yet been brought to light. The Genoese world map of 1457, of elliptical form, in the Biblioteca Nazionale, Florence, has been claimed by Professor S. Crinò as a copy or derivative of Toscanelli's map, but there are many difficulties in this identification. A chart in the Bibliothèque Nationale, Paris, has a circular inset world map in which Charles de la Roncière saw an expression of Columbus' views before his first voyage; but this association also has failed to win general acceptance.

The celebrated globe prepared by (or for) Martin Behaim at

Nuremberg in 1492, however, depicts eastern Asia and the ocean divid-
ing it from Europe in a form which closely resembles the concepts
of Toscanelli and Columbus. This parallelism has impressed all
scholars, some of whom have drawn the erroneous conclusion that
Columbus must have been acquainted with Behaim or his globe, or
that Behaim had access to Toscanelli's papers.

Professor Morison remarks that "the scale, the eastward extension
of Asia, and the narrow ocean on this globe are so similar to the false
geographical notions on which Columbus based his voyage, as to
suggest that Columbus and Behaim were collaborators"; yet he is
compelled to add that "there is no positive evidence of their trails ever
crossing," nor is it physically possible that Columbus could have set
eyes on the Nuremberg globe. The inference is inescapable that Columbus and Behaim drew on a common map-source, and that (as G. E.
Nunn suggested) "prior to his first voyage Columbus used a map of
Eastern Asia similar in concept to that Behaim presented on his globe.
It is possible and even probable that this concept had its origin with
Toscanelli."

This prototype, traces of which are found in world maps drawn
between 1500 and 1510 (figs. 5,6), may well have been a printed map.

In a brilliant paper published in 1940 Professor R. Almagià pointed
to the probability that the author of the prototype-map consulted by
Columbus was Henricus Martellus, a German cartographer who worked in Italy and was associated with the Florentine map-engraver and
publisher Francesco Rosselli. Three MS. non-Ptolemaic world maps by
Martellus, and a printed one by Rosselli, all dating from about 1490,
were known to Professor Almagià. These maps, none of which is
graduated in longitude, embrace only the land areas of Europe, Asia
and Africa, terminating in the east at the coast of Cathay; but Professor
Almagià demonstrated the close analogy, in regard to the representation
of Asia, between this group of maps and (on the one hand) Behaim's
globe and (on the other) Columbus' geographical views. He also
reproduced, from a MS. codex by Martellus, a separate map of
Cipangu, drawn in a form exactly resembling that in Behaim's globe;
and he postulated the existence of a lost "mappamundi of the Martellus
type, modified in accordance with Marinus' measures," and extended

to cover the full 360 degrees of the earth's circumference. Such a map (in Almagià's words), "gives a delineation of the world which is best adapted to Columbus' ideas, best explains the geographical premisses of all his voyages... and best accounts for his convictions and conjectures and for the projects conceived by him in the course of the four expeditions."

Two other pieces of indirect evidence suggest the existence of this prototype-map. In the *pleitos* of 1515 the son of Martin Alonso Pinzón affirmed that, in or before 1492, his father had seen in Rome a map which showed "that there, 95° to the westward (from Spain), by an easy passage, he would find between north and south a land of *Sypango*"; this plainly reflects the longitude and orientation of Cipangu in Behaim's globe and its source. Finally the inventory of Rosselli's shop drawn up in 1527 includes the *forme* (plates or blocks) of several world maps, which have been lost to sight. Since Francesco Rosselli worked at Florence from 1489 or earlier, it is not impossible that one of these printed maps was the prototype postulated by Professor Almagià as a source used by both Columbus and Behaim.

Columbus' consultation of a map which agreed, in general and in detail, with the representation in Behaim's globe not only attests his intention of sailing to "the Indies," that is, to the mainland of Asia; it also explains many passages in the *Journal*. In the second half of September 1492 they were constantly expecting to come upon islands, which were marked in a map shown by Columbus to Pinzón. Ten days later, on October 6th, Pinzón advised changing course from W to SW by W, on the assumption that Cipangu had been overshot and that they should make for the islands shown to the south by Behaim; but Columbus decided to steer straight on for the mainland of Cathay, which in the Martellus maps and the Behaim globe projects well to the east in this latitude. His identification of his landfalls betrays the influence of a map whose longitudes agreed nearly with those of Behaim. When he sighted Guanahani on October 11th, the *Journal* shows a distance sailed of 1123 leagues, or about 89 degrees, on a westerly magnetic course from the Canaries; and he at once began the search for Cipangu, which in Behaim's globe is laid down between 75° and 85° W of the Canaries. On October 24th Columbus wrote in his

Journal: "According to the globes I have seen and the world maps, (Cipangu) must be in this neighbourhood." Subsequently he identified first Cuba, and then Española, as Cipangu; and in Ferdinand Columbus' report his father missed Cipangu because he thought it extended north-south (as in the Behaim globe) instead of east-west. By November 14th Columbus, on the north coast of Cuba, took this to be the mainland of Cathay, and he wrote in the *Journal* of "the innumerable islands which in the maps are placed at the extremity of the East" — as in Behaim's globe and indeed in earlier world maps, notably Fra Mauro's and the Genoese map of 1457.

All these allusions may reasonably be referred to a printed world map of the Martellus type but graduated in longitude and extended further east than the surviving maps, to take in Cipangu and the south-eastern archipelago of Asia.

The mapping of the voyage.

Apart from the conventional representation of the Bahamas in a woodcut printed in editions of Columbus' Letter, *De insulis inuentis*, only two (or perhaps three) first-hand cartographic records of the first voyage have survived. The first is Columbus' sketch of north-west Española (fig. 2), drawn as he coasted east in December 1492 - January 1493. This precious fragment, preserved in the Duke of Alba's collection, is of infinite interest, not only as the only surviving map from the Admiral's hand and as a testimony to his skill in dead reckoning and in making a running survey of a coastline, which stands up remarkably well to comparison with the modern chart. It is also the sole extant 15th century example of the rough sketches made by pilots on voyages of discovery. The specimens of 15th century cartography which have come down to us are otherwise, without exception, sophisticated and elaborately finished work, generally with much decoration.

Their geographical content was derived, at one or more removes, from the 'roughs' brought back by the seamen; and Columbus' little sketch strikingly exemplifies the materials and the compilation methods

which went into the construction of the more polished products prepared in the cartographic workshops.

The celebrated world map signed by Juan de la Cosa in 1500 (fig.
3), and now preserved in the Museo Naval, Madrid, is such a compilation. It does not seem necessary to accept G. E. Nunn's contention that
the map was not made, or completed, before about 1508. The most
substantial evidence which he cited for this dating was the representation of Cuba as an island, for which he supposed that no proof was
available before 1508. La Cosa (it is true) was one of Columbus'
companions on the second voyage who, in June 1494, had deposed
that Cuba was a peninsula of Asia.

Columbus' desperate attempt to certify his faith in an Asiatic
discovery was to confuse geographers and mapmakers for many years;
it may explain, for instance, the duplicated delineation of Cuba – both
as an island and as a peninsula – found in the Cantino world map and
other later maps (figs. 4, 8).

Yet even in 1494 some of Columbus' shipmates preferred to believe
the Indians who spoke of Cuba as an island. It has also been suggested
that additions were made to the map after 1500; but that the whole
map is the work of a single hand is supported by the authority of Admiral S. F. Guillèn y Tato, who has devoted long and penetrating study
to it.

Yet, though we may admit the homogeneity of its authorship and
execution, the map was undoubtely – and inevitably – pieced together
from materials of diverse kinds and origin. Mr. G. R. Crone has demonstrated that it "has every appearance of having been put together from
at least two sections: the western portion, comprising the American
discoveries and perhaps the West African coasts, having been joined
to a portion of a world map resembling those of fifty years earlier which
display the influence of Ptolemy." Central and South America (as Mr.
Crone points out) are drawn on a larger scale than the rest of the map.
Built into the 'modern' position of the map are the data from voyages
of exploration or survey: those of the Portuguese in West Africa,
of John Cabot in North America, of Columbus in the Caribbean, of
the Spaniards and Portuguese in South America. For those of Cabot
and Columbus, at least, we must suppose that La Cosa made use of

such pilots' sketches as Columbus' little 'rough' of Española — rude drafts tolerably correct in outline and proportion, but in most cases doubtless lacking indications of scale, orientation, and location on the world map in terms of co-ordinates. Here is the root of the difficulty which early cartographers faced in compiling their world maps, and which we encounter in interpreting them. It explains the want of uniformity of scale in such maps, the failure to relate different parts of them coherently or correctly to one another, duplication of features, corruptions in design or nomenclature which become ever more corrupt in successive copies. Seen in this light, La Cosa's delineation of the islands and coasts explored by Columbus on his first voyage reaches a high standard of precision and accuracy, which testifies to the quality of the running surveys used by him (though he did not himself go on the voyage). His most remarkable error, which (in Mr. Crone's words) "has never been satisfactorily explained," is the displacement of Española and Cuba north (insead of south) of the Tropic, "the north coast of Cuba being shown... some 12° too far north." This was an error in compilation rather than drafting, and perhaps arose in the process of fitting together disparate materials into the framework of a world map.

The third map which may incorporate original materials from the first voyage is the work of the Turkish admiral and cartographer Piri Reis. This was drawn in 1513 from a chart said to have been obtained in 1497 from an Italian prisoner who had sailed with Columbus. While the representation of the New World — the only portion of the map that has survived — shows much confusion in the compiler's mind and does not bear comparison with La Cosa's map, Professor Morison finds details "to suggest that Piri did have a copy of a chart made by Columbus on the second voyage"; and the possibility that he disposed of similar materials from the first voyage is not to be excluded.

In conclusion, we may mention two works in which the hand of Bartholomew Columbus has been discerned, and which may embody information from his own or his brother's surveys.

The first is a MS. map of Santo Domingo, preserved at Bologna, which Dr. Vigneras associates with a letter of Bartholomew written in 1513. Secondly, there is the group of cartographic sketches in the MS. collections of Alessandro Zorzi at Ferrara and Florence (fig. 1). That these sketches were derived from communication with Bartholomew is open to doubt; in any case they were designed less as a record of exploration than as a geographer's interpretation of the relationship between the western discoveries and the mainland of Asia. As such, they will be considered below.

The cartographic interpretation of Columbus' discoveries.

The difficulties which confronted the early cartographer in working up his world map were inherent in the materials at his disposal. These difficulties did not arise only, or even mainly, from the limitations of the data which he extracted from seamen's logs and similar sources. Were the pilots' records of course and distance as good and accurate as he could wish, a twofold problem would still have remained to perplex him. First, the leagues or miles of distance noted or traversed by the explorer must be laid down on the map as a proportion of the earth's circumference, that is, converted (by an agreed factor) into degrees; and a map of the world had to account for the full 360 degrees of its circumference. Secondly, in the absence of any means of determining longitude, and therefore of accurately 'fixing' the position of any place on the earth's surface, it was extremely difficult to arrive at a correct judgement of the spatial relationship between disjunct discoveries or surveys, unless by the fortuitous identification of common landmarks in overlapping sections. These difficulties were of course enhanced when the longitudinal element predominated, as in the westward crossing of the Atlantic to make a landfall on the American coasts, or in forming an opinion of the width of unknown ocean lying between Western Europe and East Asia. In the cartographers' solution of these problems conjecture and hypothesis necessarily played a large part.

The earliest world maps to depict the discoveries in the West, including those of Columbus' first voyage, date from the period immediately after his return from the third voyage; these are the

Spanish map of La Cosa (1500), the Portuguese 'Cantino' map (1502), and the Italian 'Canerio' map drawn from a Portuguese prototype similar to Cantino. Some half-dozen MS. world maps — two of Portuguese authorship, the others by Italians using Portuguese and Spanish sources, and all but one undated — date from the years following the fourth voyage, that is about 1504-6. From 1506 onward Italian and German maps, both MS. and printed, offer varied interpretations of the American discoveries.

The elements available up to 1506 for the mapping of the West Atlantic were, first, the lands found in the North-west by the English and the Portuguese; second, the Caribbean discoveries of Columbus and the Spanish; third, Columbus' traverse of the Central American coasts in 1502-3; and fourth, the Spanish and Portuguese voyages to and along the mainland of South America. Between, and within, the sectors of known coastline were unexplored areas which the cartographer (if he was not to leave them blank) had to supply from conjecture or theory. The crucial question to be answered by a world map was the geographical relationship of the trans-Atlantic lands with those of East Asia.

Columbus' own interpretation of his discoveries, in the light of Ptolemy and Marco Polo, is illustrated in the sketch maps of Zorzi (fig. 1), which, though drawn some twenty years later, have been taken to reflect the views of Bartholomew Columbus after the fourth voyage, i. e. about 1506. In them South America appears as a great continent ('Mondo Novo') separated by a narrow strait from the discoveries of the fourth voyage, which — with the lands to the north — are identified with Ptolemy's representation of Eastern Asia. For Columbus' opinion on the discoveries of John Cabot and the Corte Reals, no cartographic evidence exists; but it is reasonable to suppose that he held them also to have a land communication with North-east Asia.

This hypothesis is graphically presented in some Italian maps, notably the printed Contarini - Rosselli map of 1506, which is discussed below.

In La Cosa's map (fig. 3), the position of the Central American strait is covered by a large vignette of St. Christopher; apart from this, the American coasts are drawn as uninterrupted from north to south. Since the mainland of Asia extends to the right-hand edge of the map, and that of North America to the left-hand edge, it is probable that the cartographer believed them to be continuous. The Portuguese mapmakers and the Italians and Germans who followed Portuguese prototypes, were more cautious. Whether the author of the Cantino map (fig. 4) accepted Columbus' identification of Cuba as the 'Cape of Asia' (recalling the easternmost promontory in the Martellus world maps) has been the subject of much debate; it appears more reasonable to associate the peninsular fragment of land, shown on the map in the approximate position of Florida, with a duplicated representation of Cuba arising from the confusion in contemporary opinion referred to above.

The peninsular 'Cuba,' with precisely the same outline, reappears in a woodcut map in the edition of Ptolemy printed at Strassburg in 1513 (fig. 8) and edited by Martin Waldseemüller. No central strait, however, is shown in this map (despite its traditional identification as 'the Admiral's map'), nor in the Peter Martyr map of the Caribbean of 1511 (fig. 7), the earliest Spanish printed map of a part of the New World, perhaps from an original by Andres Morales.

Five years earlier, the first printed map of the western discoveries, a world map drawn at Venice by G. M. Contarini had been engraved (1506) by Francesco Rosselli at Florence (fig. 5). This combined old and new elements. The delineation of East Asia, apart from one new feature, closely follows the pattern established long before by Martellus and Rosselli, tacitly rejecting the exaggerated eastward extension derived by Columbus from his short estimate of the length of a degree. In the north-east, however, a vast projection of land juts out to the eastward, its Atlantic coast being formed of the Greenland and Terra Nova discoveries by John Cabot and the Corte Reals. It can hardly be doubted that this feature reflects the interpretation of his discoveries by Cabot himself (at least after his first voyage, in 1497), and — after him — of Columbus. South of this, and separating it from the continental mass of South America, lies a broad sea passage, 50 degrees wide, within which are contained the Caribbean islands. Westward from them is Cipangu, and off the southern coast of

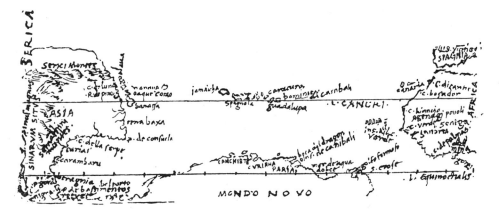

Fig. 1 Sketch by A. Zorzi of the coasts of Central and South America; based on a map by Bartholomew Columbus.

Fig. 2 Sketch of north-west Española drawn by Christopher Columbus, 1492-3.

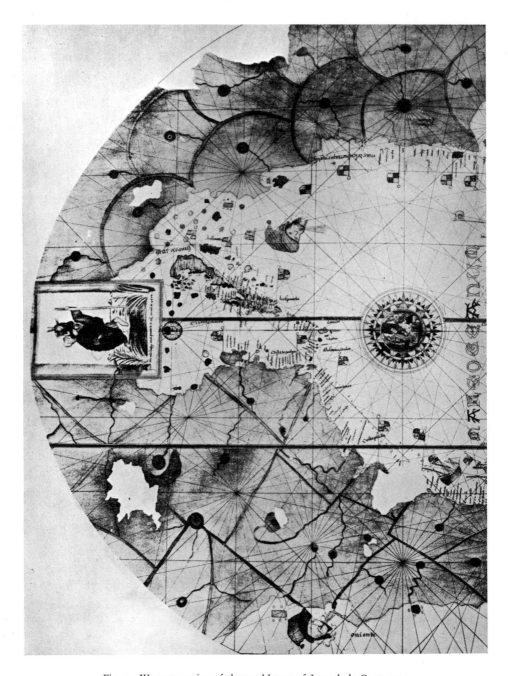

Fig. 3   Western portion of the world map of Juan de la Cosa, 1500.

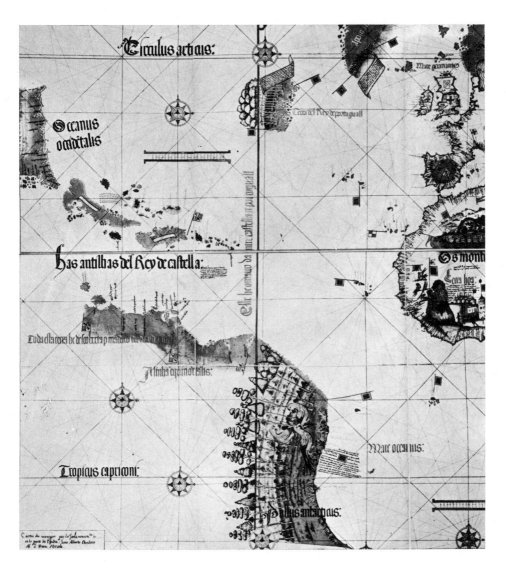

Fig. 4 Western portion of the 'Cantino' world map, 1502.

Fig. 5 Part of the world map by G. M. Contarini, engraved in 1506 by Rosselli.

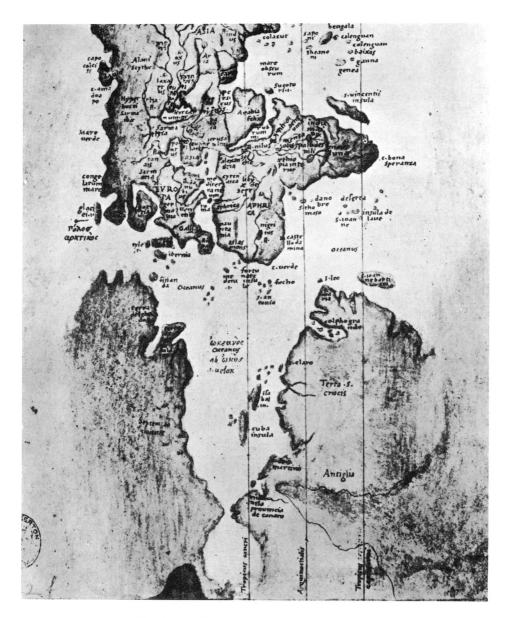

Fig. 6 Part of a MS world map drawn about 1508.

Fig. 7 Map of the Caribbean; in Peter Martyr's first *Decade of the New World*, 1511.

Fig. 8 Map of the New World; in Ptolemy's *Geographia*, Strassburg, 1513.

Hor orbis Hemiſphærium cedit regi Hiſpaniæ.

Fig. 9 The Western Hemisphere in the world map by F. Monachus, 1529.

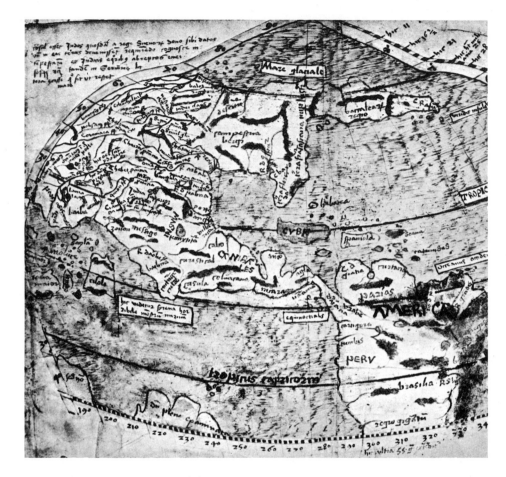

Fig. 10 Map of the Western Hemisphere drawn about 1535.

China is a conspicuous legend on Columbus' discovery of 'Ciamba' (Indo-China) — a reference to his fourth voyage. Here we have so ill-digested and adaptation of Columbus' claims to the older cartography that it has (not surprisingly) invited the suggestion that the Ciamba legend may be a later addition to the plate. A similar disposition of the land masses is found in the printed world map of Ruysch (1507) and a MS. atlas by Vesconte Maggiolo (1511).

In the woodcut world map and globe-gores by Waldseemüller, both of 1507, we find the first cartographic expression of the fact that to the three parts (or continents) of the older world maps had now been added a fourth. Waldseemüller's New World has a continuous Atlantic coastline from 50° N to 40° S, breached only by a narrow central American strait; and in drawing a western coast Waldseemüller at once foreshadowed the discovery of the Pacific Ocean and dismissed Columbus's claim to have reached East Asia.

Yet the Admiral's illusions were tenacious of life. While Columbus, at the isthmus, thought himself 19 days' journey from the Ganges, 98 days were required by Magellan for his crossing of the South Pacific. Despite this, the persistent belief in the possibility of sailing west to Asia is exemplified in maps made a decade after Magellan. Such are the little hemispheric woodcut map (fig. 9) of Franciscus Monachus (1529) and a MS. map (fig. 10), also in hemispheres, drawn about 1530-5 and preserved in the British Museum. In both maps the Pacific is bridged, across the north, by a land mass bearing the Ptolemaic names of provinces of Asia and extending eastward to the discovered Atlantic coasts of North America; and the Moluccas are laid down a mere ten degrees west of Mexico; but only the Monachus map has the Central American strait. The Columbian concept of the relationship between the continents died hard.